PRINCIPLES OF THE REFORMATION

PRINCIPLES OF THE REFORMATION

ROBERT RICHARDSON

Introduced & Edited by Carson E. Reed

Orange, California

PRINCIPLES OF THE REFORMATION
by Robert Richardson
Published by New Leaf Books

Copyright 2002 by Carson E. Reed

ISBN 0-9714289-6-4

For information contact:

New Leaf Books
12542 S. Fairmont
Orange, CA 92869

1-877-634-6004 (toll free)

Visit our website: www.newleafbooks.org

Table of Contents

Introduction, *Carson E. Reed*	7
Letter to the Reader	25
1. Distinction between Faith and Opinion	29
2. The Christian Faith	43
3. The Basis of Christian Union	55
4. Patriarchal, Jewish, and Christian Institutions	69
5. Commencement of the Christian Church	73
6. The Action and Design of Baptism	77
7. The Agency of the Holy Spirit in Conversion and Sanctification	87
8. Weekly Communion	95
9. Church Government	97
In Conclusion	100

Introduction to *Principles of the Reformation*

Poor Eyesight, Clear Vision

Dr. Robert Richardson loved his work with the monthly journal, *The Millennial Harbinger*. The detailed work of corresponding with subscribers, editing manuscripts and typesetting texts engaged this medical doctor's mind. Furthermore, writing and working with the ideas of the "current reformation" that was growing rapidly across America stirred his soul. *The Millennial Harbinger*, owned and published by Alexander Campbell, was a leading voice for this movement that we now call the Stone-Campbell Movement.

Not only did this quiet doctor enjoy the detail of this fatiguing and often grueling work, Richardson took particular pleasure in doing all he could to fairly represent the views of the prime catalyst for the movement. From March 1836, when Campbell asked Richardson to come to Bethany and help with the *Harbinger*, until Campbell's death in 1866, Richardson was one of Campbell's closest associates. Richardson attended Campbell's death and spoke at his funeral. It was Richardson whom Campbell's family asked to write a biography—an expansive two-volume tome that still stands as a definitive work on Campbell's life and career.

Unfortunately Richardson was plagued with an ongoing eye condition so that periodically he had to refrain from the work he loved best. In 1853-54, in the decade before the Civil War, he struggled through a two-year period of severe eye trouble, a period when his eyesight was so diminished that he had to step away from his editorial duties and rely on others to read and write for him.

During this time Richardson collected a series of essays he had published two and three years earlier in the *Millennial Harbinger*. Those essays offer a clear glimpse into the distinctive genius of the American Restoration Movement. Though he could not see to write, he could see the simple power of the gospel as expressed in what he called the "present reformation." In this volume, Richardson presented the fundamental principles that Campbell and others espoused. The original title was almost as long as the book itself: *The Principles and Objects of the Religious Reformation, Urged by A. Campbell and others, Briefly Stated and Explained*.

Richardson knew those principles well. He had written for the *Millennial Harbinger* for 20 years and had served as the associate editor much of that time. Richardson was a close friend; Campbell readily trusted him with the editorial work of the *Harbinger*, often leaving it entirely in his hands while traveling. A medical doctor, Richardson taught chemistry and languages at Bethany College and served as family physician for the Campbells.

Though quiet and unassuming, Richardson was highly regarded in the movement. Standing at the movement's center, among Campbell's closest associates and friends, Richardson was in the ideal place to hear, to ascertain and to interact with the core convictions that undergirded Campbell's teaching and writing. And it is from this vantage point that Richardson gathers those central convictions into a succinct book. Undoubtedly Richardson hoped that the publishing of this book would clarify the movement's goals to the larger Christian world. However, he also hoped to say something to his own constituents who were beginning to struggle with their own questions of identity.

The book was favorably received and circulated widely in the 1850s. Campbell had this to say about it:

> [*Principles*] is a concentrated view of the distinguishing traits and objects of the great work in which many of us have been engaged for many years. The author of this essay has himself been connected with [the reformation] for almost a quarter of a century, and is well posted in its history from the beginning. This tract gives a well-proportioned miniature view of it in a lucid and chaste style, and is worthy of himself and the cause. It ought to be circulated, not only among our brethren, but the religious and reflecting of all Protestant Christians.[1]

Yet, in only a few short years—1856 to be exact—a series of conflicts would erupt that would take one segment of the Restoration Movement down a path that Richardson and others simply did not want to go. Along that path, many of the principles that Campbell, Richardson and other early leaders held highly would no longer be plainly visible on the horizon.

The controversy sprang up between Tolbert Fanning of Nashville, Tennessee, and Richardson in 1856.[2] Concerned about a growing trend to understand Christianity from an extreme rationalist point of view, Richardson sought to offer what he understood to be a more moderate and biblical understanding of faith and spirituality. Fanning, a well-known preacher in the south who had just launched the *Gospel Advocate* in 1855, offered to Richardson a clear example of the dangers of rationalism. Fanning argued that one could only find the Spirit at work through the Word of God. And the way to understand and appropriate the Word of God rested on a rationalistic system anchored to the philosophy of John Locke. Thus the Bible was held captive by philosophy.

The position on the other side of the equation was illustrated by the ministry and teaching of Jesse Ferguson. Ferguson, a dynamic preacher in Nashville in the 1850s, had begun to teach and practice an understanding of the Spirit's work in people's lives that was independent of the Bible. Ferguson, caught up with popular movements in Christian groups of that day, had embraced the idea that the Spirit moved people to faith. Such a view displaced the centrality of the gospel in the process of conversion.

The ongoing debate of 1856-57 between Tolbert Fanning and Richardson led to Richardson's views being largely rejected by the southern churches. By the end of the Civil War, Campbell was dead (1866) and core understandings about the movement had become caught in the confluence of the social and economic upheavals of the war. Many of the southern churches took a fork in the river of ideas that fostered a stark rationalism devoid of the Holy Spirit. The currents that carried southern churches nearly buried the irenic and christological vision Richardson voiced in *Principles*.

What was buried? Richardson focused much of his attention on what today is called "spiritual formation." Not only was he concerned about a biblical understanding of conversion, he was concerned equally about the process of sanctification.[3] To say it differently, embracing Christ is really embracing a whole new life—a life imbued by the indwelling of the Holy Spirit. As Richardson will say in *Principles*, "The goal of the Christian faith is to be brought into direct relation and fellowship with Christ; to think of him as a person whom we know, and to whom we are known. It is to speak to him as to one who hears, and to listen to him as to one who speaks. Such, in our view, is the Christian faith."[4]

One of the things to which Richardson would call the Christian is the practice of solitude and quiet. For example, "When the soul is most abstracted from the bustle of the world, that is when it is most susceptible of communion with the spiritual system, and hence it is made an important duty, on the part of the Christian, to retire often to solitude, to fellowship of the gospel in silent meditation."[5]

Perhaps that is why the Lord's Supper figured so prominently in Richardson's practice of Christianity. Considering his collection of communion devotions, *Communings in the Sanctuary*, one finds Richardson frequently connecting the Christian with the Divine in those quiet moments at the table. Communion was not a mere ordinance, with a singular focus on remembering what God had done in the past. Communion was a place of present experience, evoking renewal for the Christian.[6]

Recovering this voice from the past and restoring Richardson's vision within the context of the developments of the 1850s offers much to present-day conversations. Could present-day Christians see what he, with limited eyesight, could see?

The Importance of Richardson

Contemporary heirs of the Restoration Movement in Churches of Christ and Christian Churches find themselves engaged in an ongoing conversation on identity. Within Churches of Christ alone, the past 15 years has seen many contributions to that conversation.[7] This conversation is important and I am glad for the efforts of many. However, I suggest that Richardson would make an excellent additional conversation partner on these issues of identity.

Consider the sources we are drawing upon in this conversation. First, we have a strong commitment to Scripture. Second, we recognize that our culture makes contributions to our self-understanding—whether we are fully aware of it or not. Third, we use the witness of our own tradition; we listen closely to the past to hear and to learn. Fourth, we make some level of commitment to the idea of God's providential leading and the work of His Spirit in shaping our future.

If these are the sources that we rely on to shape our identity and our future, then Richardson plays a vital role in at least one of those areas. In Richardson we have a clear and reasoned voice from our past that articulates with simplicity the core values of the "current Reformation." Would not his voice give us rich insight into the original vision that inspired and guided Campbell and his colleagues?

Most of us tend to look back only as far as we can see. Our understanding of church is primarily the understanding that we ourselves have experienced. Listening to Richardson lengthens the scope of understanding and offers us another solid landmark to take a sighting. In particular, *Principles* offers a concise and up-close presentation of the core values of the movement. As Richardson states in the *Millennial Harbinger* upon the release of the volume:

> The wish has been often expressed, that we had a brief, connected statement of the principles and objects of the Reformation, which would be suited to general distribution. There are many it has been urged, who will read a short treatise, who have neither time nor inclination to peruse a large volume; and there are many who will read a printed exposition of our views, who will not, or cannot, hear the preaching of our brethren. It is thought, too, that a connected view of the great principles developed in the progress of the Reformation, would give greater satisfaction to the inquiring mind, and tend better to remove prejudice and correct misrepresentation, than any occasional essays or tracts upon isolated topics.[8]

Again, the clear intent of this little volume was to give, in summary form, the heart of the movement's goals and objects. In the year following the book's publication, W. K. Pendleton, Campbell's son-in-law and an associate editor of the *Harbinger*, would announce the large volume of orders for the book. He also reiterates the book's purpose:

> This elegant little volume of 88 pages, by our well-known and esteemed friend, Dr. Richardson, is a brief but comprehensive view of the cardinal points of Christianity, as set forth and urged upon the public by our brethren. It is just such a book, therefore, as has been long asked for, and as every disciple would do well to procure.[9]

What Did Richardson See?

What does Richardson identify as the core values of the movement? Living and working with Campbell and other key leaders, Richardson sums up the distinctive principles in three ways. Those three themes form the first three chapters of the work. Let's take a look at them.

Understanding the Source of Faith
Richardson begins at an appropriate place for understanding identity; he begins with how one understands Scripture. This first chapter, entitled "Distinction Between Faith and Opinion," functions as an introduction to interpreting the Bible the way that the Bible itself calls for readers to read it. For Richardson, faith rests on Scripture's testimony. If the church fails to hear Scripture and, instead, fashions opinion to take the place of Scripture, then the movement that he is advocating will falter.

Scripture's core, which for Richardson is the gospel, can easily be distorted by human opinion and preference. Though he will say more about the gospel later in this work, he makes it quite clear that much of every denomination's distinctive tenets—those beliefs and practices that are specific to any particular group—tend to become clutter and obstruct the view of those seeking the truth of Scripture.

In fact, when it comes to opinion, Richardson is confident that diversity will always exist. Consensus will never occur on the many things that Christians argue over. Thus, echoing the Apostle Paul in the Roman letter, Richardson calls for liberty or freedom in matters of opinion. Furthermore, diverse opinions are not the source of division among people. Rather, division occurs when opinion is woven into the fabric of the church's beliefs and practices in such a way as to carry the weight that Scripture alone should carry. When presented as Scripture, opinion becomes divisive and destructive to unity and to healthy congregational life.

Since faith rests on the clear facts and truths presented in Scripture, Richardson carefully notes some foundational concepts of understanding or interpreting Scripture. Scripture must be interpreted; the Bible does not simply exist in a pure understandable state. Richardson notes how the Bible can be misdirected and misused by anyone to prove almost anything. He cares little for the proof-texting preacher, using a verse here and a verse there to prove some point or another.

For Scripture to be heard, Richardson argues that good and solid interpretive principles must be used. The interpreter must "prayerfully endeavor to ascertain the meaning of the text by the context, making the Scriptures their own expositor, and must give himself up to be led by them, instead of presuming to lead them to his own favorite and preconceived opinions, by wresting and perverting them from their true meaning and application." Richardson is calling for an interpretive process that gives due weight to the historical and literary realities of the text. Remarkably, he is also placing attention on the humility and openness that must accompany the interpreter as he considers Scripture.

Scripture, for Richardson, is not something to be controlled or manipulated to fit some doctrinal framework. Scripture has depth and mystery; interpreters would do well to honor the appropriate distance between the "glimmerings of spiritual systems far distant from our own."

Notable too is Richardson's understanding of the community for hearing Scripture. The older should teach the younger; churches should value the work of pastors and teachers. Perhaps it is this sense of community that balances what was of great importance in the middle of the nineteenth century—the value of making one's own way in the world. Richardson strongly calls for people to think and to reason. The reformation that he advocates is a challenge to simply accepting things because they have been taught in the past or because one's church has always done it that way. Richardson wants people to engage God for themselves. And the direct engagement that one can discover by going to Scripture is foundational for spirituality and for this movement.

In order to let Scripture be Scripture, Richardson also points out the movement's interest in language. The language—the very words—that a group uses to describe itself or its practices function as primary influences on people. Thus Richardson notes that the movement has made every effort to fashion its identity with biblical concepts and names. Richardson is bright enough to know that merely calling something by a biblical term does not necessarily make it biblical. However, he also knows that if a group is serious about the Bible being fundamental for its identity, then biblical terms must permeate its language.

Richardson has more defining to do of the core values of the movement. But the first chapter clears the ground for the foundation. Differentiating between what is faith and what is opinion, Richardson calls for solid biblical exegesis done with a disciple's spirit. Tradition/opinion will always shape the church, but does not form the foundation. Richardson reminds us that Scripture determines the landscape of the church's identity.

Common Christianity
If faith and not opinion serves as the basis of Christianity, than Richardson moves to carefully define faith. He understands that the Bible presents the truth and the facts of faith and when approached in Bible-honoring ways those facts and truths can be discerned. But the Bible contains much more than the material that gives rise to the core of Christian faith. Richardson notes that all Protestants understand the difference between general teachings of Scripture and those things that comprise the core of the faith.

The debate is really over what makes up the core of faith. For most Protestant groups as well as many contemporaries in the Restoration Movement, what makes up the core are a set of doctrinal truths or values. Sometimes written formally as a creed, and sometimes simply understood as the unwritten values of a congregation, those teachings or beliefs come to be bound up as the content of faith. To be a Christian one must understand and accept those doctrines. Richardson would call this point of view—dominant in his day—a doctrinal view of faith.

But how one understands faith is the radical distinguishing point of the reformation that Campbell and others were urging. For Richardson presents a very different way of understanding faith. Rather than understanding faith to be rooted in the intellectual consent to a set of doctrines, Richardson says that faith is rooted in relationship. "[T]hey suppose doctrines, or religious tenets, to be the subject-matter of this faith; we on the contrary, conceive it to terminate on a person—the LORD JESUS CHRIST HIMSELF."

Thus for Richardson, faith does not rest on correct doctrine, for doctrine is always and inevitably shaped by different denominational and cultural biases. Rather, faith rests in relationship. Taking the simple facts of Jesus' life, death, and resurrection story and thus embracing the gospel, a person enters into saving relationship with God.

The usual practice of making faith out to be an elaborate system of beliefs and practices quickly overshadows the simple design of God's heart. Indeed, Richardson argues that it is those elaborate systems of faith that fracture and divide Christians from each other. That is not to say that various doctrines and teachings are unimportant to him. However, they must be seen as secondary to "this simple faith in Christ, accompanied by its appropriate fruits."

Such a vision of faith's content is foundational to Richardson's desire for "common Christianity." If doctrinal debates and distinctive teachings could be placed in a secondary position, and if faith could be seen as rooted in relationship, then Christianity could experience the unity God envisioned. "Happy would it be for the world, if all could be induced to rest content with that 'common Christianity,' which it is the very object of the present Reformation to present to the religious community as the only means of securing unity and peace."

To understand faith in terms of relationship, Richardson believes, is not naïve. Nor does such an understanding leave open the possibility of the charge that Richardson is a sentimentalist. He makes quite clear that such a faith will be evidenced by the fruits of a Christ-shaped life. Likewise, he counters by noting that all too often a faith that is defined by its adherence to doctrinal statements can quickly erode into a mental assent that produces no living, vibrant faith. How can such an understanding of faith nurture spirituality when it has never entered the human heart?

Mental assent to doctrinal truths of Scripture, without real life, is no faith at all. "The goal of the Christian faith is to be brought into direct relation and fellowship with Christ; to think of him as a person whom we know, and to whom we are known." Faith, for Richardson, is the dynamic interplay between Jesus Christ and one who has learned the truth of the gospel and whole-heartedly embraced that truth by reliance and trust.

Such a view makes it important to know what the term "gospel" means. Does it mean everything found in the New Testament? Does it include matters of how one should worship or how a church should set up its leadership system? Or does the gospel articulate a much narrower and yet much deeper truth about the wonder and mystery of God?

Richardson takes some time to address this matter. For he was aware that it is easy for many things to slip their noses under the "gospel" tent. For him the facts of faith were clearly evidence in Jesus' life, teachings, sufferings, death, and resurrection. He cites John's purpose for writing his gospel and notes Paul's recitation of the core of the gospel to the Corinthians. "It consists of the simple story of the cross and of those facts in Christ's history which reveal him as the promised Lamb of God, who should take away the sins of the world."

For Richardson, there is really only one creed that Christians should affirm. And that creed is really no creed at all—at least in the way that creeds normally function. The one standard to which all should be called and on which all should unite in spirit is simply faith in Jesus as the Christ. One can learn it by reading the Bible or one can learn it in worship as the preacher speaks it. Either way, it is the gospel message that launches faith, forms communities, and announces salvation.

Differences about doctrine and diversity of opinion will always be present in the church. But the gospel stays the same. For Richardson, claiming our common experience in the message of the gospel was the foundation for unity—for a "common Christianity."

Unity, Not Uniformity
The third of Richardson's principles was really an extension of the second. If an active, vibrant faith in Jesus Christ lies at the core of our faith, it is also at the core of the church's unity. Richardson goes to some lengths to demonstrate Scripture's witness to the way in which the confession of Jesus Christ stands at the core of the church's identity.

This of course raises questions. Just exactly what does Richardson mean by speaking of faith in Jesus? How is faith defined? Does faith refer to mental assent or does it imply a truly engaged and repentant heart? Richard anticipates these questions and gives a detailed response. For Richardson, faith is full and robust, clearly demonstrated in word and deed. Likewise, Richardson focuses on the gospel and suggests that the gospel, rooted in facts, is a much safer place to work toward unity. To allow any doctrines or teachings to take center stage inevitably creates an environment clouded by human opinion.

The Rest of the Story

After presenting the three fundamental principles of the movement, Richardson then briefly offers observations on six themes where these principles can be evidenced in the movement. One senses, at points, the datedness of the material in these sections. That is to be expected whenever we move from principle to specific practice. Nevertheless, one finds plenty to challenge current thinking about such topics as baptism and the Holy Spirit's role in the believer's life.

With regard to baptism, Richardson articulates a theology that is well worth considering. He reminds his readers of the historical and biblical precedents for immersion and then makes a remarkable move in suggesting that immersion is an ecumenical posture to take since all agree that immersion is an appropriate, biblical form for baptism. Furthermore, Richardson carefully delineates the role of baptism as the sign or seal of what God does. Baptism does not save us; salvation is the result of Christ's sacrificial gift. Baptism "is, then, to the believer, the sign, evidence, or assurance of pardon, and not the procuring cause of pardon."

Richardson carefully follows Campbell here. Baptism is the "formal pledge" of what occurs when one receives Christ. Richardson takes this course as a way of responding to the all-too-common practice in his day, and in our own, of rooting forgiveness and salvation in feelings and emotions. Though conversion should be heartfelt and most certainly should capture the emotions, it is the work of Jesus Christ as articulated in the gospel that brings salvation, not a person's remorse.

This concern ushers in another chapter in Richardson's work. As a response to the common appeal to emotion and to the common understanding that the Holy Spirit brings people to faith and salvation, Richardson offers his understanding of the Spirit. Some among the Stone-Campbell movement were advocating that the Spirit worked only through the Word; to speak of the personal indwelling of the Spirit was wrong. However, Richardson insisted that the believer is given the Spirit and that the Spirit dwells within the heart of the believer.[10]

However, the question still remains as to what role, if any, the Holy Spirit plays in conversion. Since the gospel is God's means and power to bring about salvation, Richardson argues that it is the message of the gospel that plants the seed in a person's heart. Consistent with the principle mentioned earlier—that faith is rooted in the articulation of Jesus' death, burial and resurrection—Richardson affirms that it is the gospel that engenders salvation. Thus, the receiving of the Holy Spirit is the culmination of the gospel's ministry.

Richardson's thinking here might be helpful to us in understanding the conversion process. Certainly Richardson does not disconnect the Spirit from working through the Word to influence a person's heart. However, he does help us see that it is the clear presentation of the gospel by proclamation and by life that brings new life. This stands in stark contrast to the vague and uneasy notions of emotionalism and sensationalism as sources or signs of salvation.

Reading Richardson

Writing styles and frames of reference have changed since Richardson penned these words in his study on the second floor of his home, Bethphage. In offering this work to present-day readers, I have attempted to ease the contemporary reader into an earlier time. Sentences and paragraphs have been shortened; occasionally sentences have been reworked to clarify their meaning. I have generally resisted the temptation to change any vocabulary, so the reader may have the opportunity to learn a few new words along the way. Yet the reader will undoubtedly feel something of the spirit of the times in this work.

My hope in presenting this classic work is to bring another voice to the table to enter the ongoing discussion of our identity. Because of Richardson's close association with Campbell, his editorial work with the Millennial Harbinger, and his many years at the center of the Stone-Campbell movement, he is all the more a welcome and valued conversation partner. To give a hearing to his understanding of the movement's concept about such vital things as unity, gospel, salvation, baptism and the work of the Spirit, will offer fresh insight to current conversations. Perhaps most of all, in reading Robert Richardson, current readers will experience the mind and heart of a man who gave his entire self to the living of a simple, evangelical Christianity.

Carson E. Reed

Notes

1. Alexander Campbell, *Millennial Harbinger* (1853), 117.
2. For more details on these events see C. Leonard Allen and Danny Gray Swick, *Participating in God's Life: Two Crossroads for Churches of Christ* (Orange, CA: New Leaf Books, 2001), 39-58.
3. "As a resource for Christian growth and the development of a deepening relationship of the Christian with the Lord, Richardson's body of literature has no equal among the early leaders in the Stone-Campbell movement." Stephen P. Berry, "Room for the Spirit: The Contribution of Robert Richardson," *Lexington Theological Quarterly* 21 (July 1986), 81-90, 87.
4. *Principles*, section 3.
5. Robert Richardson, *Millennial Harbinger* (June 1851), 327.
6. Look at meditation 21 in *Communings in the Sanctuary*. "In his understanding of the Lord's Supper, Richardson in effect suggested a bridge between the Catholic Mass and the Protestant memorial; this reflects his Episcopalian upbringing. Growth in holiness, or sanctification, was a frequent theme in the writings of Robert Richardson." Berry, 89.
7. One could trace those calling for renewal and a look at identity issues back to the journal, *Mission*, in the 1960's or perhaps the work of Carl Ketcherside. More recent work would include *The Worldly Church*, by C. Leonard Allen, Richard T. Hughes, and Michael R. Weed (Abilene: ACU Press, second edition, 1991); *The Cruciform Church*, by C. Leonard Allen (Abilene: ACU Press, 1990). *The Crux of the Matter*, by Jeff W. Childers, Douglas Foster, and Jack Reese (Abilene: ACU Press, 2001) is the most recent contribution to the conversation and offers a review of some of the literature within Churches of Christ on identity (129-149).

8. Robert Richardson, *Millennial Harbinger* (1853), 296.
9. W. K. Pendleton, ibid. (1854), 232.
10. Much could be said about Richardson's views on the Holy Spirit. His work, *A Scriptural View of the Office of the Holy Spirit*, stands today as the best and fullest theology on the Holy Spirit within the Stone-Campbell movement.

Letter to the Reader

Bethany, (West) Virginia, September 1852

My dear friend,
I proceed, according to promise, to lay before you the general principles and objects of the Reformation that has been, for some time, urged upon the religious communities, both in this country and in Britain. And this I do with the more pleasure, as I know you have not given heed to misrepresentations made by its enemies who have endeavored to impede its progress. You are, as well, aware of the many evils induced by that sectarianism from which it is the great purpose of the present Reformation to relieve society.

Let me observe, then, in the first place, that this religious movement is wholly based upon the two great fundamental principles of Protestantism, namely:

The Bible is the only Book of God.
Private judgment is the right and duty of man.

All Protestants assert the truths of these propositions, and cling to them as the theory of the original Reformers, who protested against the authority claimed by priests and popes to dictate articles of belief. But it is unhappily true that the party dissensions of Protestants have insensibly led them to depart, in practice, from both these cardinal principles. In direct opposition to a most obvious deduction from the first principle, they have exalted human systems of theology to an authority equal, if not paramount, to that of the Bible. At the same time, in violation of the second of these principles, they deny to the people the privilege of interpreting the Bible otherwise than in accordance with these systems. Thus a human standard of orthodoxy is substituted for the Bible; and, by a natural and inevitable consequence, the Bible has become a sealed book to the masses, who do not, because they dare not, understand it for themselves.

This states, in a few words, the actual state of the religious community. What the present Reformation proposes is an immediate return to the broad and original platform of Christianity, as well as of true Protestantism. It urges, accordingly, the claims of the Bible alone, as the source of Divine truth for all mankind. It pleads for the exercise of man's inalienable right to read and interpret the Sacred Volume. It seeks to establish a unity of faith, instead of that diversity of opinion that has distracted religious society. It desires to restore the gospel and its institutions, in all their original simplicity, to the world. In brief, its great purpose is to establish CHRISTIAN UNION upon the basis of a SIMPLE EVANGELICAL CHRISTIANITY.

Having thus given you a general statement of the purpose of this religious movement—a purpose that cannot fail to be approved by the truly pious of all parties—I now proceed to lay before you the important distinctions and truths which have been developed during its progress. And I would also remark that, as the character of prevailing errors always determines, in advance, the issues which are made by the advocates of truth, so, certain fundamental points of great importance have been thus forced upon the attention of the friends of the Reformation. These need to be elucidated. Among these I would mention:

1. The distinction between FAITH and OPINION.
2. The distinction between what may be emphatically termed THE CHRISTIAN FAITH and doctrinal KNOWLEDGE.
3. The true BASIS FOR CHRISTIAN UNION.

Among the important subjects that have come into view during the progress of the Reformation, I invite your attention to the following:

4. The distinction between the Patriarchal, the Jewish, and the Christian dispensations.
5. The commencement of the Christian church.
6. The action and design of baptism.
7. The agency of the Holy Spirit in conversion and sanctification.
8. Weekly communion.
9. Church government.

Upon each of the above topics, I desire now to give you, as briefly as possible, the views of the Reformers.

1. Distinction between Faith and Opinion

This distinction is of the utmost importance, and lies at the very threshold of religious reformation and Christian union. Without a proper recognition of the difference between FAITH and OPINION it is impossible to make any progress in a just knowledge of Divine things, or to obtain any clue by which the mind can make its way through the perplexing labyrinth of sectarianism. Notwithstanding, however, that it is so important to distinguish between these things which are so radically different from each other, people are easily confounded. The fallible deductions of human reason are continually mistaken for the unerring dictates of inspiration, and human authority is blended with that which is Divine.

Human opinions, indeed, are the plastic cement in which partyism has imbedded the more solid yet disconnected scriptural materials of its party walls. Or to employ another figure, a theory, consisting of any number of favorite opinions, smoothly intertwined, forms the thread upon which various Scripture doctrines and texts are strung and curiously interwoven, so as to assume a form and meaning wholly artificial and unauthorized.

When men thus fail to make any distinction between the express revelations of God and the opinions which men have superadded, and when they have already committed the great error of adopting indiscriminately, in the religious system of a party, an incongruous mixture of opinions with the things of faith, the mistiness and obscurity which surround the former overspread by degrees the latter also. Hence, it has come to pass that matters of belief and mere speculations upon religious subjects are usually classed together as "religious opinions;" and when we speak of a man's religious opinions, we are constantly understood to mean, or, at least, to include, his belief.

Likewise, Divine communications themselves have lost much of the authority and respect which are justly due to them, by being thus reduced to a level with human opinions, and by the implication that they are so limited in their range of subjects, and so deficient in clearness, as to require additions and explanations from uninspired and fallible men, in order to render them intelligible and complete. The question, accordingly, is no longer, "What do the Scriptures say?" "How does it read?" or "What has the Lord said?" Rather today's question is, "what do the Scriptures mean?" What do you think? What do the standards of my church or the leaders of my party say? In opposition to erroneous views and practices, we urge—

1. That the Scriptures mean precisely what they say, when construed in conformity with the established laws of language.

2. That the Bible contains the only Divine revelations to which man has access; and that these revelations are perfectly suited, by their Divine Author, to the circumstances and

capacity of man to whom they are addressed.

3. That true religious faith can be founded upon this DIVINE TESTIMONY alone.

4. That opinions are mere inferences of human reason from insufficient and uncertain premises, or conjectures in regard to matters not revealed, and that they are not entitled to the slightest authority in religion, by whomsoever they may be propounded.

The measure of faith is, then, precisely the amount of Scripture testimony, neither more nor less. What this distinctly reveals is to be implicitly believed. Where this is obscure or silent, reason must not attempt to elaborate theories or supply conclusions, and impose them upon the conscience as of Divine authority. By the practical recognition of this principle, the theological systems and theories which have distracted religious society, are at once deprived of all their fancied importance, and consequently, of all their power to injure.

Those remote speculations; those metaphysical subtleties; those untaught questions which have occupied the minds of the religious public, to the exclusion of the all-important yet simple truths of the gospel, are at once dismissed as the futile reveries of uninspired and fallible mortals. When these are thus dismissed, the human mind is left alone with the word of God. The mind is brought into direct contact with the Divine law and testimony, from which alone the light of spiritual truth can emanate, and the mists of human opinionism and speculation no longer obscure this light.

If this distinction were duly appreciated by the Protestant world, there would be a speedy end of those controversies by which it has been so long disturbed. For it is undeniable, that there is an almost universal agreement among the various evangelical denominations, in regard to the great revealed truths of Christianity. Yet they are separated, alienated and belligerent, for the sake of certain favorite opinions, which have been decreed by their founders.

Each one admits that there exists this common Christianity, apart from denominational peculiarities, and that salvation is possible in any of these parties. However, each continues to urge its distinctive tenets, and maintain its peculiar opinions, as though the salvation of the world depended upon those alone. Human opinions and speculations, then, have demonstrated too much authority with the religious public, and are too highly honored in being made the great objects for which each party lives and labors. If then, they were clearly distinguished from the revealed truths, upon which, like parasites, many of them have grown; if they were fairly separated from all connection with the Divine testimony, from which they derive a stolen nourishment and a borrowed vigor, they would appear at once in their true character, as matters wholly foreign and insignificant, and would be allowed to droop and perish with all the bitter fruits they have so profusely borne.

It is preposterous to expect that men will ever agree in their religious opinions. It is neither necessary nor desirable that they should do so. It is nowhere commanded in the Scriptures that men should be of one opinion. It is there declared that there is "ONE FAITH," but is nowhere said that there is one opinion. On the contrary, differences of opinion are distinctly recognized, and Christians are expressly commanded to receive one another without regard to them (Rom. 14.1). As well might we expect to conform the features of the human face to a single standard, as to secure a perfect agreement of men's minds.

Hence, there can be no peace, unless there be liberty of opinion. Each individual must have a perfect right to entertain what opinions he pleases, but he must not attempt to enforce them upon others, or make them a term of communion or religious fellowship. They can do no harm, so long as they are private property, and are regarded in their true light, as human opinions possessed of no Divine authority or infallibility.

It is quite otherwise, however, when leading and ambitious spirits take them for the warp and the Scriptures for the woof from which they weave the web of partyism. The flimsy and ill-assorted fabric may please the taste of the few, while it will be despised and derided by those who manufacture an article no better from similar incongruous materials, and thus a contention is perpetuated, with which human selfishness and pride have much more concern than either piety or humanity.

It is, accordingly, one of the primary objects of the present Reformation to put an end to all such controversies, by reducing human opinions to their proper level, and elevating the word of God, as the only true standard of religious faith. Hence it was, in the very beginning, resolved to "reduce to practice the simple original form of Christianity, expressly exhibited upon the sacred page, without attempting to inculcate any thing of human authority, of private opinion, or inventions of men, as having any place in the constitution, faith, or worship of the Christian church; or any thing as matter of Christian faith or duty, for which there cannot be expressly produced a 'thus says the Lord,' either in express terms or by approved precedent."[1]

Every proposition or doctrine, then, for which there is not clear scriptural evidence, is to be regarded as a matter of opinion; and every thing for which such evidence can be adduced, is a matter of faith—a fact or truth to be believed. It may be objected here; that what may be clear to one mind may be doubtful to another. Likewise, the Scriptures are constantly appealed to, by all parties, as affording to each sufficient proof of its peculiar views, which, in each case, conflict more or less with those of every other party. This may be true, but what follows? That the Scriptures are themselves a tissue of contradictions and ambiguities? That it is impossible to determine their true meaning? No, this would deny the fundamental principles of Protestantism—the Divine origin of the Bible, and the right of private interpretation. For God could not be the author of a volume of this character. Moreover, the right to interpret the Scriptures presupposes the ability to comprehend them.

The facts involved in the above objection may be readily accounted for, without impugning either the Divine origin or the intelligibility of the Bible. They are such as must necessarily occur when men adopt false rules of interpretation, or come to the Scriptures with minds already biased in favor of particular views.[2] The intelligibility of the Bible is not absolute, but relative, depending as much upon the state of mind of him who reads it, and the method he pursues, as upon the clarity of the book itself. All Protestants assert that the way of salvation is clearly defined in the Sacred Volume, so as to be plain to the most ordinary comprehension. If, then, erroneous views were formed from it, the cause is to be sought, not in the Bible, but the mind of the errorist himself.

He comes to the Scriptures as an advocate of preconceived opinions or doctrines, to seek for proofs and arguments by which to sustain these views; and not, as a sincere inquirer after truth, to engage in a process of careful investigation, and with a mind prepared to follow where ever the truth shall lead. Hence it is, that all errorists and parties holding sentiments the most discordant, have recourse alike to the Bible for their proofs. They seek not for the truth that is in the Bible, but for proofs of the errors with which their minds are previously imbued—for something to sustain the particular system to which they are inclined.

To them the Bible is a mere storehouse of arms and ammunition for partisan warfare. It has no well-defined plan or purpose of its own, but is merely a collection of proof-texts, from which any one is at liberty to select whatever may appear to suit his purpose, without respect to the context, or the laws of interpretation applied to all other writings.

Thus it is that the Bible answers the purposes of all parties equally well. As with the mirror of the Arabian tale, each one can see in it only what he wishes to see; and as each party wishes to see only itself, the Divine mirror reflects to its view no other image. A man would not be more surprised to see, in the glass before which he stands, the image of his enemy, instead of his own, than would be the advocate of one party to find in the Bible the views of an opposite sect.

It must be evident, that to treat the Bible thus, is to grossly abuse the most precious gift of Heaven, and to sustain, by a mere pretence of Divine authority, a system of partyism and contention wholly incompatible with the express purpose of Christianity, and the conversion and salvation of the world.

He who would understand the Divine communications must study them with the humility and docility of a child. He must prayerfully endeavor to ascertain the meaning of the text by the context, making the Scriptures their own expositor, and must give himself up to be led by them, instead of presuming to lead them to his own favorite and preconceived opinions, by wresting and perverting them from their true meaning and application.

Thus the one, who will devote himself to the study of the Bible, will not long remain either in ignorance, error, or doubt, as to the great matters of faith and duty. It is distinctly affirmed in the Book itself, that "the Inspired Scriptures are profitable for all things; for doctrine, for reproof, for correction and instruction in righteousness, that the man of God may be perfect, and thoroughly furnished unto every good work." If, then, the believer may be made perfect and be thoroughly furnished, what needs be more? Most assuredly, if the Book of God appear in any case to fail thus to enlighten the mind and direct the conduct, we may in vain expect that any volume from fallible and uninspired men could supply the deficiency and secure these objects.

To acknowledge that there are certain difficulties in regard to some matters of Holy Writ is but to concede the depth and vastness of its themes, and the deficiency of fallen man in his powers of comprehension, and in his aptitude to receive spiritual truths. Unquestionably, there are some subjects too mysterious in their nature to be clearly explained in human language; some too great to be completely grasped by a finite mind; many too remote from the ordinary range of human thought, to be distinctly apprehended by the most discerning intellect.

For example, in the natural heavens we have bodies so remote that they appear but as faint nebulae. We have stars that can scarcely be distinguished by human vision from those which cluster around them. So have we, in the Book of God, glimmerings of spiritual systems far distant from our own, whose relations to us we may never comprehend in our present state of being. Such must necessarily be the case in regard to communications concerning the Divine Creator and the things of an infinite, unseen, spiritual world.

These are subjects to be reverently pondered and contemplated only so far as, upon the heavenly scroll, we may discover their outline, or discern their more salient points. These are not things about which men may dogmatize; into which they may vainly and presumptuously intrude; or in regard to which they may insolently excommunicate and anathematize each other.

To admit, further, that the Bible will not be at once equally clear to all minds, even in regard to matters actually developed in it, is only to confess that men are unequal in capacity, in spiritual mindedness, and in devotion to the means of biblical knowledge. Within the Bible itself this is so. Peter said of Paul's Epistles, that it contains "some things hard to be understood;" which, nevertheless, may be understood through diligent study and proper use of the means of biblical interpretation.

Scriptural knowledge is, therefore, progressive, and will vary in different cases, and in the same person, at different periods. There will be always babes, young men, and fathers, in scriptural learning. Hence, there is opportunity to comply with the apostolic injunction that the elder should teach the younger and that Christians should edify each other. Likewise, we recognize the use of pastors and teachers, who, in the exercise of their functions, promote the growth and edification of the church.

How different, however, from this primitive state of the Christian church with its mutual spiritual edification and growth and its common yet individual interest of the Divine communications, is the imbecile condition of perpetual and hopeless pupilage in which congregations wait for the weekly explication of some fragment of Scripture called a "text." No member presumes to edify himself or others by his own researches. No one ventures to trust himself to the Word of God or to advance a single step in scriptural knowledge, lest he should ignorantly miss the path prescribed by church authority and become entangled in the snares of error!

The truth is, that the great mass of Protestants is just as effectually debarred, by clerical influence, from the exercise of the right of private judgment in matters of religion, as are the Romanists themselves by priestly prohibition. They have no confidence in the intelligibility of the Bible, or in any views that they may take from it. An individual, having once in his life exercised the right of private judgment, not in regard to the things taught in Scripture, but in choosing between the systems and tenets of different parties, and having adopted the particular system which he prefers, will for ever after rest content with the orthodoxy of his opinions, and give himself little concern about what may be contained in the Scriptures of Truth. One who unites with the church of Rome, must thus far, at least, exercise the right of private judgment in choosing between conflicting claims, and shows a similar indifference to the Holy Volume of inspiration.

Indeed, it is difficult to conceive why, on his own principles, the sectary should make a proper use of the Bible. He may, indeed, read it as a pastime or as a task; he may even feel a certain interest in its historical details, or be more or less impressed with its sublime imagery and powerful diction; but for truly religious purposes it can avail him nothing. Confident that his favorite creed-makers have secured the treasure for his use, he cares but little for the casket, which he thinks himself unable to unlock. Believing them to have traversed the whole area of revelation, settling authoritatively all difficult questions, guarding all its essential truths and unfolding in a few brief sentences all the deep and hidden mysteries, what inducement can he have to do research or bring his mind into direct communication with the Word of God?

In this Reformation, however, it is a fundamental principle that every one shall take his religion directly from the Bible, without the intervention of popes or priest, councils or assemblies, or any of the creeds that they have framed. With us, every thing in religion must have a Scripture warrant, and human authority is regarded as wholly incompetent to the decision of any question that may legitimately arise in regard to the great matters of faith and duty.

Whatever rests upon a Divine warrant is a matter of FAITH. Whatever subordinate and collateral questions may exist which have not this warrant are MATTERS OF OPINION, which each one is at liberty to entertain according to his own pleasure, and to which no one, from the very nature of the case, can attach any importance. Nor is it to be imagined that any doctrine or sentiment can be justly entertained under the title of an opinion that will conflict with or nullify any portion of Scripture. Where the Bible speaks, there is no place for any opinion; and if any one hold a view which contravenes any declaration of Holy Writ, this is not an opinion, but actual DISBELIEF of so much of the Word of God as is thus contradicted and opposed.

In entire harmony with these views, it is regarded as of the utmost practical importance to speak always of religious matters in the exact language of the Bible. All those unscriptural terms and expressions, of which the modern sectarian vocabulary almost wholly consists, are, accordingly, discarded as conveying ideas more or less foreign from the Bible, and as being in no case so accurate and appropriate as the language of Scripture. It is true, that Bible terms themselves may be misunderstood or misapplied, if the context is not carefully examined—especially if a religious theory or favorite practice be in question. But when an individual is unable to express his religious sentiments, without using unscriptural expressions it is prima facie evidence that his religious views are not in the Bible. For if they were, he could certainly state them in the exact language of the Sacred Volume.

Such is the reciprocal influence of words and thoughts that any change in the language employed by the inspired writers is to be regarded with suspicion. It can not be supposed possible to have a restoration of the simple original gospel of Christ and the primitive institutions of Christianity with its primitive modes of thought and action, without a return to the primitive modes of expression also. The names and many of the institutions of the different sects, as well as their modes of speech, are alike utterly unknown to the Bible.

As for those who take part in the present Reformation, they desire to have nothing to do with any thing in religion that is not at least as old as the books of the New Testament. In aiming to restore and obey the simple primitive gospel and its institutions, and to give to these Bible things their Bible names, they desire to assume no other titles than those originally given to the followers of Jesus. Thus such terms as DISCIPLES OF CHRIST, CHRISTIANS, THE CHURCH OF CHRIST, or THE CHURCH OF GOD, etc. are regarded as scriptural and to be used interchangeable, according to circumstances.

I hope that I have been sufficiently explicit upon the distinction to be made between faith and opinion. But now, as faith springs from the Divine testimony, and will be co-extensive, so to speak, with the knowledge that any one may have of that testimony, the question arises, "How great must be the extent of this faith, in order to entitle an individual to be received to church membership?"

In other words, "How much of the Bible must he have explored and comprehended, before he makes a profession of Christianity?" Must he have examined the whole Divine testimony, in regard to all the subjects of which it treats? Or, are there particular points or doctrines, to which his attention may be restricted, and in regard to which alone his faith may be properly inquired into and tested? Or, to shorten the question, "What is the 'the faith,' 'the truth'—the belief which 'sanctifies' and 'saves' the soul?" Our views of this I shall now proceed to give you.

Notes

1. *Declaration and Address of the Christian Association of Washington*, p. 4.

2. Among the most prolific sources of error in religion is the practice of taking isolated texts of Scripture, and giving to them a meaning and application never intended by the writers. Of this nature is the fallacy employed by the Westminster and other confessions, in the numerous Scripture references ap-pended to each article of the creed. These are taken as proofs by those who are too indifferent or too indolent to ascertain, by an actual examination of the context, that the passages so referred to have, in most cases, little or nothing to do with the particular matter to which they are applied. There are not wanting many, however, who, even with the passages before

them, would regard the least allusion to the subject as abundant proof of any proposition which might be offered in regard to it. Hence the easy credulity of those who believe the doctrines of the text-proofing preacher.

To obtain the true sense of Scripture we must carefully inquire:
1. What is said?
2. Who says it?
3. To whom or of whom is it spoken?
4. Under what circumstances was it said?

We must always take the language in its proper connection with what precedes and what follows.

2. The Christian Faith

A thorough knowledge of the Bible is not regarded by any of the sects as an essential prerequisite to a profession of faith. However, all agree that there are certain fundamental points that must be believed, and which, taken together, constitute what is termed orthodoxy.[1] To extract these from the Bible has been the great business of councils and assemblies, which smelting, as it were, in their party furnaces, the ore of Holy Writ, have obtained, as they imagined, from it, the pure and precious metal. This they have then mixed with the requisite portion of alloy to give it hardness; and having stamped it with their own theological image and superscription, have issued it as the only standard coin in the realm.

Each party, however, disagreeing as to the characters which should distinguish this precious metal, have, unfortunately, obtained a different product, and we have, consequently, in circulation, as many standards as there are parties. Thus it would puzzle the most skilful assayer in the theological mint to determine their relative values.

Nevertheless, we certainly concur with the rest of the religious world in making a distinction between what is properly and especially "the faith," or the Christian faith, and a general belief and reception of the Divine testimony, contained in the canonical books of the Old and New Testaments. But we differ from all the parties here in one important particular, to which I wish to call your special attention. It is this: that while they suppose this Christian faith to be doctrinal, we regard it as personal.

In other words, they suppose doctrines, or religious tenets, to be the subject-matter of this faith; we, on the contrary, conceive it to terminate on a person—the LORD JESUS CHRIST HIMSELF. While they, accordingly, require an elaborate confession from each convert—a confession mainly of a doctrinal and intellectual character, studiously elaborated into an extended formula—we demand only a simple confession of Christ—a heartfelt acknowledgment that Jesus is the Messiah, the Son of God.

The Christian faith, then, in our view, consists not in any theory or system of doctrine, but in a sincere belief in the person and mission of our Lord Jesus Christ. It is personal in its subject, as well as in its object; in regard to him who believes, as well as in regard to that which is believed. It consists of simple facts, directly connected with the personal history and character of Jesus Christ as the Messiah and the promised Lamb of God who takes away the sins of the world. It is personal in its object, leading to personal regard and love for Christ, and a personal interest in his salvation. It consists not in definitions; neither does it embrace the litigated questions of sectarianism. It contains not one, much less five cardinal points of speculative theology; nor does it inflict upon the believer, for his sins, forty articles save one.

The gospel of salvation, indeed, would be ill-fitted to be preached to every creature, illiterate or learned, if it consisted, as some imagine, of those ponderous bodies of divinity, and intricate systems of theology, which have oppressed the energies and entangled the movements of the Protestant world.

Indeed, the great error of Protestants and the great cause of all their schisms has been the attempts to supersede this direct personal reliance upon Christ, by a mere intellectual assent to a set or system of tenets. True, they do by no means deny this personal trust or faith in Christ. But the natural working of the whole machinery of a party, so far as it is peculiar and denominational, tends to lead the mind away from this simple faith to a false confidence in mere human opinion, intellectual abstractions, and in outward forms.

Many are lulled into a false security, trusting to the orthodoxy of their belief, and mistaking a zeal for human opinions as a meritorious earnestness for saving truth. Others substitute an extravagant admiration of the leading men and favorite preachers of their denomination for the love of Christ.

Thanks, however, to the power of the gospel itself, this tendency of the systems of the day has been checked in individual cases. Some have gazed, in silence and in secret, upon that face "marred"; that form insulted; those bleeding wounds of the Just and Holy One who "offered himself without spot to God," and have, in humble hope yielded to him alone their confidence and love.

Such individuals are found in all parties, and they recognize each other as being fellow-heirs of the grace of life, and as having a common interest in the great Redeemer. It is, indeed, this simple faith in Christ, accompanied by its appropriate fruits, which constitutes that "common Christianity" which is admitted to exist in all parties, independent of party peculiarities. And such an admission assigns to these peculiarities their true character—mere excrescences upon Christianity. They have no power to save and serve as the very means of perpetuating division. Happy would it be for the world, if all could be induced to rest content with that "common Christianity," which it is the very object of the present Reformation to present to the religious community as the only means of securing unity and peace.

I am aware, that it will be difficult for those who have been accustomed to regard the Christian faith as an assent to a particular set of tenets, to recognize this simple belief in Christ as sufficient to admit an individual to the blessings of Christianity. If, however, they will fully consider the scriptural import of this faith in Christ, they will perceive an extreme simplicity that adapts it to all minds; it necessarily involves and includes all the conditions of salvation.

It is to be noted, that to believe in Christ is not simply to believe what Christ says; that is, to receive as true whatever may be regarded as the teaching or doctrine of Christ. This is the very inadequate and erroneous view which we have been combating, which mistakes an intellectual assent to the deductions of reason from Scripture premises, or even to the express dictates of inspiration, for a personal and direct reliance upon Christ himself.

Again, to believe in Christ is not merely to believe that there lived a person bearing that name. Yet there are multitudes that seem to have no higher idea of the Christian faith than this, and no better knowledge of the term Christ than to suppose it a mere personal appellation. But the word Christ is not a name. It is an official designation. The name Jesus, given by express command of God, is itself significant, and the addition of the word CHRIST, with the definite article, which is often expressed and may be always supplied, furnishes the titular and qualifying expression which denotes the peculiar character of the person.

He is not Jesus Christ, as an individual thus named and surnamed. He is JESUS THE CHRIST. These propositions are totally different. The former might be to us of no peculiar moment; but the latter expands itself over the past, the present, and the future, and involves in it the eternal destinies of the human race.

Yet, to believe the person to whom this title is applied to be what the title really imports is to believe something concerning this person of a most important and far-reaching nature. However, even this would fall short of constituting the Christian faith, if this conviction be supposed unconnected with that trust and direct reliance upon this person which would be justly due to him in the office and character thus assigned to him.

Whether or not it be possible for any one fully to understand the import and bearings of the sublime proposition that Jesus of Nazareth is the Christ, and truly to believe it, and yet, at the same time, to entertain the proposition as a mere intellectual conviction, without giving up the heart to him in humility, penitence, and love; to trust and confide in him as the only Savior, and the anointed King of kings, is a question which I deem it unnecessary here to consider. For certain it is, that if it be possible for any one thus to separate, in point of fact, words from thoughts, thoughts from things, or things from the emotions they are fitted to excite, and to believe this proposition as a mere doctrine, tenet, or mental abstraction, such a one does not possess the Christian faith.

To believe in Christ, is to receive him in all the glory of his character, personal and official; to trust in him in all the relations which he sustains to us, as our Prophet, our Priest, and our King; to behold in him our only hope and refuge; and renouncing ourselves, our own self-confidence, our righteousness, and every vain device, to lean on him only as our stay, and to look to him only as the "Lord our Righteousness," as our salvation and our life.

It is not merely to believe what is said of him as the Son of God; as the Son of Man, as living, dying, rising, reigning, returning. Believing this one comes to trust in him as our Savior, to walk with him as our teacher, our friend. One comes to realize his gracious presence with us, and to discern his footsteps in the path we tread.

The goal of the Christian faith is to be brought into direct relation and fellowship with Christ; to think of him as a person whom we know, and to whom we are known. It is to speak to him as to one who hears, and to listen to him as to one who speaks. Such, in our view, is the Christian faith. The Christian faith is not a trust in definitions, doctrines, church order, apostolic succession or official grace. Nor does the Christian faith rest in opinions or dogmas, whether true or false. Rather the Christian faith rests in a sincere belief of the testimony concerning the facts in the personal history of the Lord Messiah, accompanied by a cordial reception of him in his true character as thus revealed to us and an entire personal reliance upon him for our salvation.

That this simple trust in Jesus, and nothing else, is really and truly "the faith," will be clearly seen by any one who will examine the Scriptures upon the subject. He will there find:

1. That the history of Jesus of Nazareth is related to us—his birth, miracles, teachings, sufferings, glorification—for an express purpose. Our attention is called to the fulfillment of the ancient prophecies for that same purpose—to produce this faith. I need only here refer to the close of the testimony of John, where he expressly declares this to have been the object: "And many other signs truly did Jesus in the presence of his disciples, which are not written in this book; but these are written that you might believe that Jesus is the Christ, the Son of God."[2]

2. That Jesus himself declares, that "God so loved the world that he gave his only begotten Son, that whosoever believeth in him should not perish, but have eternal life." And he announces, also, on the other hand, that it is the rejection of this faith that occasions condemnation. "He that believeth not is condemned already, because he has not believed on the name of the only begotten Son of God." And many other passages might be quoted of the same purport.

3. That he commissioned the apostles "to go out into all the world and preach the gospel to every creature," declaring that he that believed and was baptized should be "saved," and that he that believed not should be "condemned." Now, "the gospel" is simply the glad tidings concerning Christ; that "he died for our sins according to the Scriptures, was buried and rose again, according to the Scriptures" (1 Cor. 15.3,4). It consists of the simple story of the cross and of those wonderful facts in Christ's history, which reveals him as the promised Lamb of God, who should take away the sins of the world. To

believe these facts is to receive Jesus as the Christ, the Son of God, and the Savior of men.

4. That the apostles, in fulfilling this commission to preach the gospel, gave to those whom they addressed, a concise statement of these facts in Christ's history, and presented the evidence on which they rested. Their goal was to produce in the minds of their hearers this belief in Jesus as the Messiah, and requiring no larger faith than this, and no more extended knowledge than this to introduce their hearers into the Kingdom of Christ.[3]

5. That this faith in Christ is that which is expressly enjoined in order to receive salvation. See the address of Paul and Silas to the Philippian jailer (Acts 16.31): "Believe on the Lord Jesus Christ, and you will be saved." Or Philip's declaration to the eunuch (Acts 8.37): "If you believe, with all thy heart, you may." And the eunuch's satisfactory reply, "I believe that Jesus Christ is the Son of God." Again John says, "This is his commandment, that we should believe on the name of his Son Jesus Christ, and love one another, as he commanded us."

6. That it is this faith that not only introduces the believer into the Christian institution but enables him to maintain his profession and sustain him against the temptations of life. "Whosoever shall confess that Jesus is the Son of God, God dwells in him and he in God." Again, "Whosoever is born of God, overcomes the world; and this is the victory that overcomes the world, even our faith. Who is he that overcomes the world, but he that believeth that Jesus is the Son of God?"

But I need not multiply quotations to show that a sincere belief in Jesus as the Christ, the Son of God, is emphatically and truly the Christian faith, and the only faith that can lawfully be demanded in order to admit one to Christian privileges and church fellowship. This is the CHRISTIAN'S CREED, and the only creed to which any one may be justly called upon to subscribe. And this being so, all other creeds and confessions are at once nullified and repudiated, as without Divine authority, and mere inventions of men, leading the mind away from Christ, and from a direct and personal reliance upon him, to mere intellectual conceptions, abstract propositions, and human opinions. Or, if other creeds do not lead to opinions and intellectual abstractions, then they at least lead to subordinate truths, collateral questions, and remote conclusions. Such things belong not immediately to what is properly the Christian faith, but to the subsequent chapter of Christian knowledge.

Hence, even upon the hypothesis that the religious formularies of doctrine now in vogue contain nothing but truth, we deny the right of any one to complicate the simplicity of the Christian faith in this manner, and to demand, in advance, a degree of knowledge and experience in the child. A degree, which, in the very nature of things, can be expected only in one who has attained to the stature of a man in Christ Jesus.

It will appear, then from the above, that, while we regard the whole Bible as the only repository of true knowledge in religion, and as the volume which is to occupy the mind and heart of the Christian student, we consider that particular portion of it which is immediately concerned with Christ's personal history and ministry, as that which is to be presented to the unconverted world as embracing the subject matter of the Christian faith—the simple gospel of Christ.

This may be either read in the book itself, or presented by the living preacher. "Faith comes by hearing, and hearing by the word of God." It is a plain and simple narrative, the truth of which was confirmed by signs and miracles; "those demonstrations of the Spirit" which attended its introduction, and which were then faithfully recorded, in order to accomplish the same purpose in all future ages. It is this gospel that is the "power of God for salvation, to every one who believes it." It is not a power of God—one of the methods which God employs to save; but it is emphatically the power of God for salvation; the only revealed way in which God can, in consistency with his own attributes, justify and save the sinner.

It is the cordial belief of this love of God, thus manifested in the life, death, resurrection, and glorification of Christ, which reconciles man to God, which overwhelms the soul in penitence and contrition for its offences, and, through the influences of the Holy Spirit, produces entire renovation of heart and reformation of character. In brief, it is Christ himself who is thus made to us "wisdom" and "righteousness," "sanctification and redemption."

Notes

1. "Orthodoxy," as Warburton wittily observed, "is my doxy, and heterodoxy is another man's doxy."

2. Nothing contributes more to a correct view of Scripture than a knowledge of the particular design of each of its main divisions. John, as here quoted, expressly states the immediate purpose of his "gospel" or testimony to be to produce the belief that Jesus is the Christ, the Son of God. That Matthew, Mark, and Luke had the same object in view is perfectly apparent from the nature of the facts they relate and the application they

make of them. The four "gospels" are concurrent testimonies, and their concurrence is additional evidence of the truth of the facts recorded. Those facts are selected and arranged with special reference to their force and fitness as proofs of the great proposition above mentioned.

Again, in the "Acts of the Apostles," we have a special purpose, viz. To show how the apostles fulfilled the commission they had received from Christ, in opening the kingdom of heaven. 1st, To the Jews, as related in the second chapter. 2nd, To the Samaritans, as reported in the eighth chapter. 3rd, To the Gentiles, as recorded in the tenth chapter. The call of the latter being still further exhibited in Paul's travels and labors. Many other matters also of great importance are stated, as the descent of the Holy Spirit, the proceedings of the primitive churches, etc. So, also, the Epistles have a particular purpose. The letter to the Romans develops, in a continuous argument, the great doctrine of "justification by faith," in opposition to the Jewish view of the efficacy of the works prescribed by the Mosaic law. The letter to the Hebrews presents also a continuous argument to show the superiority of Christ to Moses and of the Christian institution to the Jewish institution. A clear view of the design of each epistle is thus a key to its interpretation.

3. Take, for example, Peter's discourse in Acts 2: "You men of Israel, hear these words: Jesus of Nazareth, a man approved of God among you by miracles and wonders, and signs which God did by him in the midst of you, as you yourselves also know; Him, being delivered by the determinate counsel and foreknowledge of God, you have taken, and by wicked hands have crucified and slain; whom God has raised up, having loosed the pains of death, because it was not possible that he should be held by death.... Therefore, being by the right hand of God exalted, and having received of the Father the promise of the Holy Spirit, he has brought for this, which you now see and hear.... Therefore, let all the house of Israel know assuredly that God has made that same Jesus, whom you have crucified, both Lord and Christ."

The effect of this discourse was, as we are told, that three thousand persons were pierced to the heart and converted to Christ. Or, take, in the following chapter, Peter's address to a different audience: "The God of Abraham, and of Isaac, and of Jacob, the God of our fathers, has glorified his Son Jesus; whom you delivered up, and denied him in the presence of

Pilate, when he was determined to let him go. But you denied the Holy One and Just, and desired a murderer to be granted unto you, and killed the Prince of Life, whom God had raised from the dead, whereof we are witnesses." The result of this was, we are told, that about five thousand men "believed." "Howbeit, many of them which heard the word believed; and the number of the men was about five thousand." Or take the first discourse to the Gentiles: "The word which God went unto the children of Israel, preaching peace by Jesus Christ, (He is Lord of all). That word, I say, you know, which was published throughout all Judea and began from Galilee, after the baptism which John preached; how God anointed Jesus of Nazareth with the Holy Ghost, and with power; who went about doing good and healing all who were oppressed of the devil, for God was with him. And we are witnesses of all things that he did, both in the land of the Jews and at Jerusalem; whom they slew and hanged on a tree. Him God raised up the third day and showed him openly; not to all the people, but unto witnesses chosen before by God, even to us, who did eat and drink with him after he rose from the dead. And he commanded us to preach unto the people, and to testify that it is he that was ordained to be the judge of the quick and dead. To him give all the prophets witness, that, through his name, whosoever believes in him shall receive remission of sins." Or, again, take Paul's preaching at Antioch in Acts 13.17-41, etc.

3. The Basis of Christian Union

Every one will agree that the true basis of Christian union is the CHRISTIAN FAITH. All the parties assert this, but, unfortunately, each one adds to that faith, or, rather, substitutes for it, human opinions and matters of doctrinal knowledge not immediately connected with salvation. They refuse to receive each other because they do not happen to agree in these opinions and doctrines, while, at the same time, they may hold in common what really constitutes the Christian faith.

This Christian faith, as we have seen, is simply belief in Christ, as he is presented in the gospel, and it is concisely engrossed in the great proposition that Jesus is the Christ, the Son of God. No one can comprehend the terms of this proposition without having before his mind the whole Christian faith in its subject matter. The predicate, "the Christ the Son of God," if understood, implies a knowledge of God and a belief in him, and presents to view not only the official character of the Messiah as the Christed or anointed Prophet, Priest, and King of whom the prophets spoke, but also his personal character or divinity as the Son of God. The subject, "Jesus," is an expression which can be comprehended only as it involves an acquaintance with the personal history of Jesus of Nazareth, and, consequently, of the great facts which constitute the gospel.

The whole proposition thus presents to us—Jesus as the Son of God—the Christ, or anointed One, whom God has appointed to be our Teacher, our Redeemer, and our King. His precepts are the ones we are to listen; through whose precious blood and intercession we are to obtain forgiveness; by whose word and Spirit we are to be sanctified, and by whose mighty power we are to be rescued from the captivity of the grave.

As in nature the lofty spreading oak was originally contained in the acorn, or, rather, in a single cell of that acorn, upon which were impressed all the nature and laws of development which distinguish the mighty monarch of the woods, so it has pleased God to wrap up, as it were, in a single proposition, that vast remedial system which may overspread and shelter, in its full development, the whole assembled family of man. In it is presented the simple word or gospel which is most appropriately termed "the good seed of the kingdom," and which, when it grows up and is fully matured, produces fruit unto eternal life.

It is the same Infinite Wisdom that has dictated the arrangements both of nature and religion. In both, apparently the most simple means produce the grandest results. In both, the processes are slow and gradual. It is "first the blade, then the ear; then the full corn in the ear." Nowhere is the ground so torn with sudden violence that the full-grown oak may be planted, or that it may receive into its bosom the spreading roots of grain ready for the sickle.

"The Kingdom of God," says the great Teacher, "is as if a man should cast seed into the ground, and should sleep and rise night and day, and the seed should spring and grow up he knows not how." It is the simple gospel that is sown in the heart, and not, as sectarians imagine, complete and elaborate systems of theology.

It is with this proposition and its proofs, that God first meets the sinner, and it is in its cordial reception that the latter finds the grace and mercy of God. Oh! That the sectarian world could thus contemplate this beautiful simplicity of the truth as originally presented by Christ and his apostles, and, adopting it as the true ground of Christian union, could be induced to forsake for it those confused and complicated systems which have no power either to save sinners or to unite saints.

The above observations address themselves to those who may, at first view, suppose this basis of union to be too narrow and to contain too little, while, in truth, it contains all, and is the very germ from which the whole Christian institution proceeds. But there are cavilers who may object, on the other hand, that it contains, or rather implies, too much—involving questions about which men will differ. They will say that there are not only in the above proposition itself, but in the preliminary knowledge which it supposes, many matters about which men may and do disagree; and that this formula, then, however simple and concise it may appear, may nevertheless give rise to debate and division. To this I would reply that we might as readily look for the giving of a law by which men could be justified, as expect to obtain any basis of union which men, in their pride of opinion and love of controversy, may not make a ground of disunion.

It is true that men have started a great many questions respecting the nature and attributes of God; about the character and sonship of Christ; the method, object, and extent of the atonement, etc., etc. And it is true that some of the warmest religious disputes are upon these very topics. But these are either untaught questions, with which we have nothing to do, (for we have no business with any religious questions which are not rooted in the Bible,) or they are vain speculations upon matters utterly beyond the reach of the human intellect, or, lastly, they are sublime truths which can be fully unfolded only in the chapters of Christian knowledge and experience, and in regard to which we have no right to demand, in advance, even that amount of knowledge which the Scriptures themselves furnish when fully explored.

All these disputes, in short, are about doctrines, intellectual conceptions, and abstract truths. However, as we have endeavored to show, the Christian faith has respect to facts, by which we do not mean truths delivered, but things really and actually performed and attested by witnesses. There are, indeed, some general truths which we must suppose the mind to have received before it could possibly apprehend the gospel facts. For instance, it must have been admitted the being of God. But all such fundamental and elementary truth here required is either self-evident or of such a nature that it cannot be supposed absent from the mind. Hence the Bible nowhere attempts to prove the existence of God. It begins by declaring the fact that "God created the heavens and the earth," but it takes for granted the elementary truth that there is a God.

Now, the great proposition on which the Christian Institution rests, affirms, in like manner, a simple matter of fact, involving the same elementary truth, which requires no new proof, and can justly give rise to no controversy. It is either the fact that Jesus is the Son of God or it is not. Upon this question rests the whole Christian fabric, and it is one which is not to be proved by reasoning from abstract principles, but by the testimony of God himself and the evidence of such other facts as are pertinent to the case. Such, accordingly, are the very proofs which are supplied in regard to this great basis of Christianity, which, like the sun in the heavens, is placed far above all those controversies which have so beclouded the religious parties as almost wholly to conceal its splendor and intercept its life-giving beams.

It is in this great fact that the Lord Jesus Christ himself is presented to us in his true and proper character, that we may so receive him and trust in him. He is, indeed, the Sun of Righteousness, the radiating and attracting center of the spiritual system, shedding light on the heavens and on the earth—upon the things of God, and the nature, duty, and destiny of man.

In accepting the above proposition, then, we take Christ himself as the basis of Christian union, as he is also the chief cornerstone and only foundation of the church. To demand, instead of this, as a profession of faith and basis of union, an exact knowledge of remote points of Christian doctrine, is as unscriptural as it would be irrational to prohibit men from enjoying the light and warmth of the natural sun until they had first attained a high proficiency in astronomy, and were able to determine the movements and magnitudes or the remote planets and inferior satellites of the solar system.

Neither do we, on the other hand, at all concede that this great fact may be confounded with anything else in the Divine testimony, or that its splendor may be at all diminished by comparison with any one or all other facts presented to the mind. It stands alone in all its sublime grandeur, amid the revelations of God. There is nothing, indeed, which may be justly compared with it. All other propositions in Christianity are subordinate to this, and can be rendered visible only by the light that it sheds upon them. Allow me here to offer a few additional considerations from the Scriptures, which will serve to give a just view of the position that this fact occupies in the Christian institution.

1. The proposition, which asserts it is a DIVINE ORACLE, in a specific and peculiar sense, for it, was announced by the Father himself from heaven. It is seldom, indeed, that God has directly addressed himself to men, and when He lays aside the ordinary methods of communication and presents himself, as it were, in person, to speak to mortals, we may be sure the communication is one of the most transcendent importance. Such was the case when, at the baptism of Jesus, in presence of the assembled multitude upon the banks of the Jordan, there cam a voice from heaven, saying, "THIS IS MY BELOVED SON." Such was also the case at the transfiguration, when the same declaration was repeated to the chosen disciples, in presence of Moses the giver, and Elijah the restorer of the law, with the significant addition, "HEAR YE HIM."

2. This proposition is the rock upon which Christ himself declared he would build his church. I refer here to Matthew 16.13-19, where we are told that Christ, after inquiring what were the conclusions of the people in regard to him, and receiving, in reply, a statement of their various opinions, put to his own disciples the question, "But who do you say that I

am?" To this Peter promptly replied, "You are the Christ the Son of the Living God."

This is a most remarkable passage, and is, of itself, quite sufficient to show the position that this declaration occupies. It was because Peter was the first to make this direct confession of Christ, that the Savior honored him by committing to him the keys of the Kingdom—the privilege of opening the gates of this kingdom to the Jews and also to the Gentiles. He fulfilled that office as described in Acts 2 and 10. This, of itself, indicates the high value attached to this declaration. But we are not left to judge of its importance merely from the honor awarded to him who was the first to make it. Christ himself expressly declares here, referring to Peter's confession of his Divine sonship, that upon this rock he would build his church, and that against it, thus founded, the gates of death should not prevail.

Now, it must be evident to every mind, that the foundation of the church can be the only basis of Christian union. The church is but the general assembly of saints, and the basis on which it rests must, of necessity, by the ground of union and communion of its members. And whatever is a sufficient basis for the whole church, must, of course, be sufficient for each individual member of that church. Upon that basis they can be united together as a church of Christ, and upon no other basis. "Upon this rock," says Jesus, "I will build by church." "Other foundation can no man lay," says Paul, "than that which is laid, which is Jesus the Christ," who was announced in his divine and proper character in the above declaration.

3. This is the "good confession" which Christ himself "witnessed" before his judges, and for which he was condemned to be crucified. During his ministry, he had forbidden his disciples

to tell any one that he was the Messiah, reserving to himself to make this confession at this awful moment, before the great tribunal of Israel. When all other evidence had failed his enemies, and he was adjured by the High Priest to say if he was the Christ, the Son of God, he replied in the Hebrew style of affirmation, "You have said." "What further need," cried the High Priest, "have we of witnesses; behold we have heard his blasphemy." And they answered, "He is worthy of death." Can any thing more clearly display the true character of this great proposition, than the fact that Jesus thus honored it by dying for it? He was himself thus laid as the foundation corner-stone of the church of the Living God.

4. But finally, it is abundantly evident from the Scriptures that it was this very confession that was made by those who, during the ministry of the apostles, were admitted to the institutions of the gospel and the fellowship of the church. I have already referred you to the discourses of the apostles, which have all the same object—to produce the belief, and, of course, the acknowledgement of this great fact. I need only refer again to the detailed case of the Ethiopian eunuch, who, after JESUS was preached to him by Philip, demanded baptism. Philip said, "If you believe with all your heart, then you may." And he answered, "I believe that Jesus Christ is the Son of God." We see, then, that as Christ declared he would build his church upon this rock, and was himself laid as its foundation-stone, so the apostles and evangelists proceeded to build upon this tried foundation, as living stones, those individuals who, through this simple faith in Christ, were made alive to God.

From what I have already said, you will doubtless fully comprehend our views of what constitutes the true basis of

Christian union. A truth-loving mind is not disposed to cavil, and knows how to select the most favorable point of view from which to judge correctly of the questions at issue.

Sectarians, however, are a race of cavilers. Partyism narrows the mind and perverts its powers, so that it becomes incapable of appreciating or even perceiving the beauty or excellence of truth. Self-satisfied and confident in its own infallibility, it has no love of progress, and desires no change, so that it necessarily opposes itself to any overture that can be made to heal the scandalous divisions that exist, and restore the original unity of the church. It will, doubtless, start many groundless objections to the above basis of union, which are unworthy of notice.

There are some, however, sometimes presented, which, as they involve misrepresentations of our views, I will here briefly consider. For example, sometimes one will ask, do you propose, then, to receive persons into the Christian Church upon a simple confession of their belief in Christ as the Messiah, the Son of God, without repentance or change of heart, or even baptism? Would you receive any one to communion with the church upon such a declaration, without any inquiries as to the sense that he attaches to the expression "Son of God," or in respect to his feelings and experience of the grace of God in his heart? May you not thus receive and fraternize with those who are Unitarian or Sabellian in faith, or mere formalists in practice?

As a general answer to all such objections, I might say that it is enough to know that any course of procedure has a Divine warrant, in order to adopt it without the slightest fear of any consequences that may ensue. But more particularly, I would say in regard to the reception of those who would attach a peculiar or Unitarian sense to the words of the above proposition, that such a perversion is a natural result of preconceived theories and speculations, which lead men to explain away the plainest statements of Scripture or wrest them away with specious glosses. Remember that according to the fundamental principles of this Reformation, all such speculations are to be abandoned, and the word of God itself is to be taken as the guide into all truth; there is not the slightest room for apprehension.

And this is, thus far, fully confirmed by our experience. I presume there is not a religious body in Christendom which renders a more true and just honor to the Lord Jesus Christ, or receives with a more sincere faith all that the Scriptures declare concerning him. With us, he is the Son of God, in the strict sense of these words. He is the Word that was in the beginning, which was with God and was God. He is the Word by whom all things were made; in him was life, and who became flesh and dwelt among men, revealing his glory—the glory as of the only begotten of the Father, full of grace and truth.

He is the brightness of the Father's glory and the express image of his person. In him dwells all the fullness of the Godhead bodily. He is Immanuel, God with us, who, having brought in an everlasting righteousness, made an end of sin by the sacrifice of himself. And having for us triumphed over death and the grave, he has been invested with all authority in heaven and in earth, and has taken his seat at the right hand of the Majesty in the heavens, where he must reign until all his enemies are subdued, and from whence he shall come the second time, in his glory, with all the holy angels, to judge the world.

In short, whatever character, office or relation, is assigned to the Father, to the Son, or to the Holy Spirit in the Sacred Scriptures, we most sincerely acknowledge in the full sense and meaning of the terms employed. It is for the express purpose of securing the truth, the whole truth, and nothing but the truth, upon this most momentous subject, as well as upon all others in religion, that we desire to adhere to the exact language of the Bible. We repudiate all that scholastic jargon that theologians have presumed to substitute for the diction of the Holy Spirit, for such jargon mystifies, perverts, dilutes, and enfeebles the sublime revelations of God.

With regard to the other inquiry, respecting repentance and a change of heart, we do certainly expect every one who presents himself for admission into the church, to exhibit satisfactory evidences of both. By the word repentance we here imply much more than a mere sorrow for sin, which may often exist without producing any amendment of heart or life. Judas is thus said to have "repented;" and persons are often, in this sense, sorry for their actions, because they feel or fear the consequences which flow from them, or because of some transient and superficial impression, and not because they have realized the true nature of sin, the purity and perfection of the Divine character, and their own unworthiness.

In the original Greek of the New Testament, two different nouns, metameletheia and metanoia, are employed to express these two different conditions. However, in the English version these two words are, unfortunately, always rendered by the same word "repentance." Thus, the distinction that is made in the original does not appear in the translation. Both words occur in 2 Corinthians 7.10, which reads: "For godly sorrow works repentance to salvation not to be repented of." We have here what appears to be a play upon words, as Dr. George Campbell observes, which was far from the design of the apostle, who in the first part of the sentence uses the word metanoia, but at the close employs the other expression. The former denotes not only a sorrow for sin, but also such a conviction of its true nature as leads to amendment of life. The latter signifies merely that regret or uneasiness of mind that may exist without any change of conduct. The first involves both repentance, in this limited sense, and what we embrace in the word reformation. So to approach, perhaps as closely as our language will admit, to the sense of the apostle, we would render the passage thus: "For godly sorrow works a reformation unto salvation, not to be repented of." It is this most comprehensive expression which is employed by Peter, in Acts 2.38, when, in addressing those who believed his annunciation of Jesus as the Messiah and were pierced to the heart, he commanded them to "reform."

It is this sincere penitence, accompanied by change of conduct, the proper fruit of reformation, which in our view constitutes the only true evangelical repentance. We do not, however, imagine, as many seem to do, that the sinner can, by this repentance, establish any claim upon the Divine mercy. Neither do we suppose that by any sort of penance he may acquire merit in the sight of Heaven, or perform works of supererogation to be placed to the accounts of others. Likewise, we are just as far from believing that God is yet to be reconciled to the sinner, or that the prayers and tears and penitence which either the sinner, or others in his behalf, may offer, can possibly render God more propitious, or more willing to save.

We do not take such a view of the gospel as to perceive any room whatever to call upon GOD to be reconciled to men. On the contrary, we regard the reconciliation as fully accomplished on the part of God through the death of his Son. It is MEN who are now required to return to God, who is "in Christ reconciling the world unto himself." Hence says Paul in 2 Corinthians 5.20: "WE are ambassadors for Christ: as though God did beseech you by us, we pray you in Christ's stead, be reconciled to God." There is not, indeed, a more unscriptural or anti-evangelical conception, than that the sinner can do any thing, either to atone for his own sins, or induce the Deity, by an act of special or extraordinary grace, to interpose in his behalf, and to renew his heart independent of the gospel. We have no fellowship with any theory that makes the word of God of no effect, or represents God as requiring to be moved with greater love for man than that which he has manifested in the gift of his Son. We are accustomed to place far more reliance upon a willingness to hear and to obey the Lord's commandments, as an evidence of a change of heart, than upon all those dreams, visions, and animal excitements, on which many are taught to depend for the proof of their conversion.

The heart is changed when we love God. It is a DIVINE philosophy, that "WE love God because he first loved us." And "by this we know that we love God, if we keep his commandments." A sincere belief of the gospel will produce its appropriate fruits, and it is by these alone that we can scripturally recognize the sincerity of the faith and the repentance. Individuals may confess Christ in word, but in works they may deny him. They may call him Lord, but refuse or neglect to obey his commands. And when such persons unite themselves to the church, we find, in their case, the Scriptures no less profitable for reproof and correction, than they are, in that of the true believer, for "instruction in righteousness."

4. Patriarchal, Jewish, and Christian Institutions

Having dwelt so long upon the leading principles of the Reformation, it will now suffice to present a very brief statement of the results proceeding from the practical application of these principles. Among the earliest of them was the discovery that Christianity is a distinct and peculiar institution, complete in all its parts, and requiring no addition from any system of religion previously established.

No clear and just distinctions had ever been made between the different religions presented in the Bible. On the contrary, such were the confused notions of the religious public. Christianity was supposed to be merely an emendation of Judaism, as the latter was, in turn, regarded as an improvement upon the more simple system of the patriarchal age. In short, it was supposed that the Bible contained but one religion. It was usual to attempt to cover the confusion of thought and the practical incompatibilities arising from this view, under the notion that this religion was presented in three dispensations—each of which was a modification of the one that preceded it. Thus, in the form called Christianity, we were to find, as it were, a mere change of external rites, or a substitution of one thing for another, without any radical or essential difference in principle, administration, or authority.

Hence, in different parties, we have so much of Judaism incorporated with Christianity, from the external pomp of Temple-worship and the simulated robes of the Aaronic priesthood, to the more serious commixture of the discordant introductory principles—mere fleshly descent, and a living faith in Christ.

It is not to be denied, indeed, that the great principles of religion and morality have been the same in all ages, and that the essential means of access to God and of acceptance with Him, have remained unchanged since the faith of Abel. But it is equally true, that for special purposes, connected with the development of the Divine character and government, there have been established, at different periods of the world's history, peculiar institutions, administrations, or economies, which differing as they do in the most important particulars, it is essential to distinguish from each other, in order to comprehend any of them.

We recognize, then, as remedial systems: First, the PATRIARCHAL INSTITUTION, which continued from the fall of Adam to the Divine mission of Moses. Second, the JEWISH RELIGION, which remained in force from Moses until the coronation of Jesus as Lord and Messiah. Third, the CHRISTIAN ECONOMY, which continues from that time to the present, and is never to be superseded by any other.

The Patriarchal institutions of religion were adapted to the early period of the world. The head of the family was its officiating priest. Religious knowledge rested upon tradition, with special revelations to those who were distinguished for their faith and piety. This age had, accordingly, its own proportion of Divine truth; its own special promises; its peculiar faith; and its appropriate religious rites.

The Mosaic system, also, had its own specific purposes to sub serve. It was a theocracy; a peculiar form of government; a civil polity, as it contained the political regulations of an entire nation. Yet it was, at the same time, a religion,[1] embodying in its precepts, and shadowing forth in the various types and symbols of its elaborate ritual, the most sacred truths, and revealing the Divine character in new and most important lights. As an institution, indeed, it was so peculiar and so different from any other that has ever existed, that there is not the slightest difficulty in determining its nature and defining its boundaries.

Especially is it to be distinguished from Christianity, in whose spiritual and literal truths the Judaism's carnal and typical observances found their destined fulfillment; and to whose simple faith and all-embracing amplitude, its outward ceremonial and restricted boundaries gave place. Differing thus in its very nature and in its principles of membership, the Jewish institution contrasts with Christianity in all essential points. In its covenants, its promises, its mediator, its priesthood, its laws, its ordinances, and its sanctions, it is exhibited upon the sacred page as wholly diverse from the gospel institution.

How indispensable it is, then, to a just view of Christianity, that these important differences, which are so distinctly noted by the apostle to the Gentiles, in his letters to the Hebrews and Galatians, should be fully understood and acknowledged. Certainly, the simple gospel of Christ should be freed from the corrupting admixture of Judaism, with which it is still contaminated in the minds of so many of the religious public!

Note

1. Paul, in addressing the Galatians (1.13, 14) says: "You have heard of my conversation in time past in the Jew's religion." In Paul's view, then, Judaism was a distinct religion from Christianity.

5. Commencement of the Christian Church

The same obscurity that has rested upon the landmarks of the various Divine institutions of which we have spoken, has naturally enveloped the origin of the Christian Church as well. Some suppose its foundation to have been laid in eternity; others, concluding to await the creation of man, make Adam its first member; others postpone it to the days of Abraham; and not a few make it coequal with Moses. To any one, however, who will trust the Scriptures upon the subject, nothing can be plainer than that the Christian Church commenced its formal existence on the day of Pentecost that immediately succeeded Christ's ascension into heaven. I need here only notice some of the scriptures from which this is abundantly evident.

In the first place, in order to show that it did not originate before Christ's personal ministry, it will be sufficient to quote the express language of Christ himself, who, in reference to Peter's acknowledgment that he was the Messiah, says: "On this rock I will build my church." He here uses the future tense—"I will build." Thus, the church was not yet founded upon this rock, its only true foundation. Christ himself, indeed, became the chief corner-stone of this spiritual edifice, which is said to rest also upon his apostles and prophets, who were the earliest members and supports of the church.

There are, indeed, some passages that seem to imply that the church had already an existence during the ministry of Christ on earth. These must, however, in harmony with others, which are more definite, and with the facts of the case, be understood as spoken prospectively. For example, we see this style in the institution of the Lord's Supper, in which Christ speaks of his blood as shed, before the event actually occurred. It is true that the body, so to speak, of the church, was prepared during Christ's ministry; and this body was, on the day of Pentecost, quickened by the impartation of the Holy Spirit, just as God first formed the body of Adam, and afterward "breathed into his nostrils the breath of life."

Just so, also, in the types of the Jewish religion, the tabernacle and the temple were first prepared, and then the Shekinah or Divine Presence took up his abode in them as the necessary sanction, without which all their religious ministrations would have been unacceptable and invalid. It was not until every thing was finished, and the ark of the Lord placed beneath the cherubims, that fire descended from heaven to consume the offered sacrifice, and that the glory of the Lord filled the temple.[1] Without the presence of the Holy Spirit, the Church of Christ could have no life, nor power to exercise its functions, nor could it be recognized as distinctly and formally established in the world.

Hence the disciples were commanded to "tarry at Jerusalem" until they should be "endued with power from on high,"[2] and they were then to proceed to preach the gospel among all nations, "beginning at Jerusalem." This was in accordance with the prophecies of Isaiah and of Micah, that "out of Zion should go forth the law, and the word of the Lord from Jerusalem."[3]

So that we have thus distinctively fixed both the place and the time at which the Christian institution should commence. It was then and there only that all things were prepared. Christ had there offered himself as a sacrifice for the sins of the world, and had thence ascended into the true holy place, to appear in the presence of God, where, having been exalted and crowned "a Prince and a Savior, to grant repentance and remission of sins," and having, also, received of the Father the promised Holy Spirit, he communicated, upon that eventful day, those gifts and life-giving energies to his waiting disciples, by which the church was quickened into being, and enabled to assume, for the first time, its distinct and appropriate character and functions. Hence thousands were on this day converted, as related in the second chapter of Acts; and it is in the close of this same chapter that we, for the first time, find the church distinctly spoken of as an existing institution. "The Lord," we are told, "added daily to the church such as were saved."

We find, then, that the three things required in order for the establishment of the Christian Church were all present upon the day of Pentecost referred to, and not earlier. A body of disciples was then prepared. The Lord Messiah having humbled himself to the death of the cross, was then exalted, and glorified, and constituted head over all things to his church, "which is his body, the fullness of him who fills all in all." And lastly, this glorious head then imparted to this body that Holy Spirit which he himself received of the Father, in order that his church might be thus fitted to discharge its appropriate functions, and that its members might be all animated by one Spirit, and be thereby united to each other and to God, through him. Thus, as the mission of Jesus was to the Jews, that of the Holy Spirit was to the church,[4] and that of the church to the world.[5]

We find, further, that the first Christian Church was that at Jerusalem. So that as the spiritual Jerusalem is the "mother" of all believers, the literal Jerusalem is the mother of all the churches of Christ on earth. Thus, the pretensions of the Roman hierarchy, based upon the antiquity of the church afterward founded at Rome, are false and unfounded, as they are arrogant and presumptuous.

Notes

1. 2 Chron. 5.7-13; 8.1.
2. Luke 24.49; Acts 1.4.
3. Isaiah 2.63; Micah 4.2.
4. Jesus says to his disciples: "I will pray the Father and he shall give you another Comforter—even the Spirit of Truth, whom the world cannot receive." John 14.17; 15.26.
5. "You are the salt of the earth." "You are the light of the world." Matt. 5. "The house of God, which is the church of the living God, the pillar and support of the truth." 1 Tim. 3.15.

6. The Action and Design of Baptism

The originators of the present religious movement were, all of them, from Pedobaptist parties. They were united together as a distinct society, for the purpose of effecting Christian union, upon the principles which I have laid before you, and had been thus engaged for a considerable time before their attention was especially called to the subject of baptism. The question was at length brought up by a member, who expressed a doubt as to the lawfulness of infant baptism, inasmuch as he could find neither precept nor precedent for it in the Scriptures. To this it was replied, that if the practice had not a Divine warrant, they would be obliged to relinquish it, as according to their principles, they could regard nothing as a matter of faith or duty, for which there could not be produced clear scriptural evidence.

Soon after, it was again objected, that there could be found no Divine authority for the rites of sprinkling or pouring, as modes of baptism, since the word baptism itself, as well as the language in connection with it, and all the circumstances attending the recorded baptisms of the new Testament, evidently indicated that an immersion in water was the action originally known as baptism.

Upon this, the society immediately entered upon an examination of the whole subject. After a careful investigation, continued for a number of months, it was finally decided that there was not to be found in the Bible the slightest authority for the baptism of any one who was not a believer. That an immersion in water was evidently the action originally indicated by the term, and practiced by primitive Christians.

Such conclusions, under the circumstances of the case, opposed, as they were, to the previous views and practices of those concerned, and to the popularity of the cause in which they were engaged, will weigh not a little with the candid and reflecting, as additional evidence of the force of truth, and the futility of those customs which, from tradition, convenience and carnality, have been substituted for the ordinance of Christian baptism. The views thus adopted were immediately put into practice, and have continued unchanged to this day—frequent discussion and the severest scrutiny having only tended to confirm and extend them.

It would be quite unnecessary for me to present to you here the scriptural evidences to show either that a believer is a proper subject for baptism, or that immersion is baptism. No Pedobaptist authority ever denied either of these propositions. On the contrary, they are both universally admitted to be true. The whole controversy has been upon the questions: whether infants, who are incapable of believing are fit subjects? And, whether sprinkling, pouring, anointing, or any other action than an immersion in water, may be justly considered as a literal and true baptism?

It belongs to those who take the affirmative of these questions, to prove them. This they have often attempted to do, but with what success I must leave you to judge. Suffice it to say, that the Church of Rome claims to have delivered infant baptism as a tradition to Protestants, and candid Pedobaptist Protestants admit that the practice rests wholly on church authority. They confess themselves unable to bring any direct scriptural evidence in support of it.[1] Of course, as we deny that mere tradition, or any assumed church authority, is a proper foundation on which to build religious institutions, we can have nothing whatever to do with the practices in question.

I wish, however, to call your attention for a moment, to the aspects of this matter, as it stands related to Christian union. Apart from the intrinsic merits of the questions which respect baptism itself, it will be seen that in adopting the action of immersion, which all grant to be valid baptism, and in admitting the believer, who is allowed by all to be a proper subject, we offer no impediment whatever to Christian union. We introduce no litigated or doubtful questions. We adopt that in which all are already agreed. We require no one to act contrary to the dictates of an enlightened conscience. We demand nothing more than what the word of God clearly and unequivocally enjoins. In this point of view, then, the position that the Reformation has assumed upon this subject is eminently antisectarian and conciliatory.

Nor, if we may regard the plain declarations of Scripture as worthy of universal acceptation, or the popular creed as fair exponents of the views of the different religious parties, are we less catholic in the sentiments that we hold in regard to the design of baptism, viz. That it is for the remission of sins.[2]

To the believing penitent, we regard it as an assurance of

actual forgiveness, or, as clearly expressed in the Westminster Confession, "a sign and seal of remission of sins." It is, then, to the believer, the sign, evidence, or assurance of pardon, and not the procuring cause of pardon. This is a distinction that it is important to make, since the very same language is used in reference to the design of Christ's sacrifice. He says himself, "this is my blood, shed for the remission of sins." Nay, we find that salvation or pardon is, in the Scriptures, attributed to various other causes such as faith, grace, obedience, or repentance. But who does not see, that while salvation may be thus attributed to any one or all of these, it cannot be supposed to be connected with them all in the same sense?

In fact, is it not obvious, that while, as all admit, the blood or sacrifice of Christ is the procuring cause of our salvation, it is through faith, repentance, and baptism that he may hence be said to believe unto salvation, or to be baptized for the remission of sins, as the means of attaining to the actual and personal enjoyment of the salvation purchased by the death of Christ? All these means of enjoyment are necessary, but each in its proper place and order, and, among them, baptism is especially distinguished as the remitting ordinance, or formal pledge of pardon—a position which, from its symbolic and emblematic character, it is so eminently fitted to occupy.

Thus it is called the "washing of regeneration," through which we are introduced into the kingdom of God, and we are said to be "buried with Christ by baptism into death," to be "baptized into Christ's death," and so forth. The simple fact that we put on Christ in baptism, is abundantly sufficient to show that we must find in it a pledge of pardon. For he who puts on or receives Christ must also receive his salvation. No one can be in Christ and in his sins at the same time. "If any man be in Christ, he is a new creature; old things are passed away; behold, all things are become new." It is in immersion, accordingly, that the penitent believer puts off "the body of the sins of the flesh" and becomes a partaker of the benefits of the death of Christ, and it is in it also that he is raised again with him "to walk in newness of life."

It must be acknowledged, however, that while we thus most cordially assent to what both the Scriptures and the creeds expressly say, that baptism is for the remission of sins, the sects at present existing (if we except, perhaps, the Episcopal) do by no means assent to it, and, upon this subject, believe neither the Scriptures nor their own creeds. This seems to be owing chiefly to the fact, that a particular theory of spiritual operations, which has gradually almost entirely monopolized the minds of the Protestant community, makes the assurance of pardon to rest on certain feelings, or upon what thought to be supernatural visions, or special spiritual communications.

The attempt is thus made to transfer the office of baptism, as the remitting ordinance, to vague, emotional, or mental impressions. To effect this purpose, the connection of baptism with the remission of sins is totally denied. The unfortunate result is that not a single individual in any of these parties is taught to regard baptism practically, as a pledge or assurance of pardon.

It is greatly to be deplored, that a mere theory of conversion should have so engrossed the attention of the religious world, and that it should have exercised so deleterious an influence upon the minds of the unconverted, as to lead them to neglect and disparage positive Divine institutions, and the appointed means through which the assurance of pardon is actually bestowed.

Nevertheless, we would not, by any means, desire to underrate the importance of the work of the Holy Spirit, or of a change of heart. No one can be born again, unless he is born of Spirit as well as of water, and no one can enjoy the remission of sins who is not thus regenerated. But we cannot consent that the peculiar object or purpose assigned to baptism in the Scriptures should be transferred to any internal operations or feelings, without Divine authority. In the present instance, the Scriptures do, in various forms of speech, assert the connection between baptism and remission, but they nowhere teach that any mental impressions, visions, or extraordinary visitations, are to be regarded as evidences of pardon. Nor is it anywhere said, that men are to receive the Holy Spirit for the remission of sins. This brings me, however, to the consideration of spiritual influence, which is next in order.

Notes

1. As one among many evidences that candid Pedobaptists confess themselves unable to bring forward direct scriptural evidence in support of infant baptism, we present the following extract from the August number of the *North British Review*, a most able work, conducted, we believe, by Sir David Brewster, the son-in-law of Dr. Chalmers, and others. In this extract, infant baptism is acknowledged to rest on church authority alone, which was also the view of Coleridge. Although this foundation may be satisfactory to those who believe that the church has power to alter Christ's institutions, or to establish new religious rites, it leaves infant baptism without any support whatever, in the view of true Protestants, who will admit no authority in religion but the word of God:

"The baptismal service is founded on Scripture, but its application to an unconscious infant is destitute of any express scriptural warrant. Scripture knows nothing of the baptism of infants. There is absolutely not a single trace of it to be found in the New Testament. There are passages which may be reconciled with it, if the practice can only be proved to have existed, but there is not one word which asserts its existence."

"Baptism appears in the New Testament avowedly as the rite whereby converts were incorporated into the Christian society; the burden of the proof is entirely on those who affirm its applicability to those whose minds are incapable of any conscious act of faith."

"The truth, then, is clear. The language of Scripture regarding baptism implies the spiritual act of faith in the recipients. When infant baptism is now spoken of, the necessary modification must accordingly be made in applying language used by Scripture concerning spiritual baptism only. Inextricable confusion has been the inevitable consequence, when language used of adults, of persons possessed of intelligence, and capable of spiritual acts, was gratuitously applied to unconscious infants; and it cannot be a matter for wonder, that a totally new conception of the ordinance should have been created by such a perversion. So great was the difficulty felt to be by Luther, who retained infant baptism, and assumed that the language used of baptism in Scripture applied to the baptized infant, that in order to fence out priestly superstition, he imagined that God, who bestowed regeneration, bestowed, also, by a direct miraculous act, that intelligent faith which the spiritual nature of Christianity demanded. Our age is not likely to acquiesce in such a resolution, but it bears witness to the just perception which Luther had of the impossibility of applying to infants, without a modification somewhere, the scriptural language regarding baptism."

2. It cannot be denied that Peter, on the day of Pentecost, commanded the believing penitents to be baptized for the remission of sins, nor that Ananias said to Paul, "Arise and be baptized, and wash away they sins;" nor that the same connection between baptism and remission is asserted in many parts of Scripture. Neither can it be denied that the Episcopal Church, in its larger creed, puts into the mouth of the believer these words: "I acknowledge one baptism for the remission of sins;" nor that in its 27th Article (on baptism) it says:

"Baptism is not only a sign of profession and mark of difference, whereby Christian men are discerned from others that are not christened;

but it is also a sign of regeneration or new birth, whereby, as by an instrument, they that receive baptism rightly, are grafted into the church, and the promises of the forgiveness of sins, and or our adoption to be the sons of God by the Holy Spirit, are visibly signed and sealed."

Neither can it be denied, that in the practical application of these views the minister is instructed to say to those presenting themselves for baptism:

"Beloved, ye hear, in this gospel, the express words of our Savior Christ, that, except a man be born of water and of the Spirit, he cannot enter into the kingdom of God. Whereby ye may perceive the great necessity of this sacrament, where it may be had. Likewise, immediately before his ascension into heaven, (as we read in the last chapter of Saint Mark,) he gave command to his disciples, saying, Go ye into all the world and preach the gospel to every creature. He that believeth and is baptized shall be saved; but he that believeth not shall be damned; which also shows unto us the great benefit we reap thereby. For which cause, St. Peter, the apostle, when upon his first preaching of the gospel, many were pricked at the heart, and said to him and the rest of the apostles, Men and brethren what shall we do? Peter replied and said unto them, Repent and be baptized everyone of you for the remission of sins, and ye shall receive the gift of the Holy Ghost; for the promise is to you and to your children, and to all that are afar off, even as many as the Lord our God shall call. And with many other words exhorted he them, saying, Save yourselves from this untoward generation. For, as the same apostle testified in another place, even baptism does now save us, (not the putting away of the filth of the flesh, but the answer of a good conscience toward God,) by the resurrection of Jesus Christ. Doubt ye not, therefore, but earnestly believe that he will favorable receive these present persons, truly repenting, and coming unto him by faith, that he will grant them remission of their sins and bestow upon them the Holy Ghost; that he will give them the blessing of eternal life, and make them partakers of his everlasting kingdom."

Nor is it to be denied, that the *Westminster Confession of Faith* expresses itself to the same effect, as follows:

"Baptism is a sacrament of the New Testament, ordained by Jesus Christ, not only for the solemn admission of the party baptized into the visible church; but also to be unto him a sign and seal of the covenant of grace, of his engrafting into Christ, of regeneration, of remission of sins, and of his giving up unto God, through Jesus Christ, to walk in newness of life; which sacrament is, by Christ's own appointment, to be continued in his church until the end of the world."

Nor, finally, can it be controverted, that while the Methodist Discipline adopts, in substance, the Episcopal form, the Baptist creed says:

"Baptism is an ordinance of the new Testament, ordained by Jesus Christ, to be unto the party baptized a sign of his fellowship with him in his death and resurrection; of his being engrafted into him; of remission of sins, and of his giving up unto God, through Jesus Christ, to live and walk in newness of life."

But I need not multiply quotations from the Scriptures, to show that baptism is for the remission of sins, or that it is in this ordinance that an individual is born of water, according to the declaration of Christ in John 3.5. Neither is it necessary for me to make further extracts from the creeds to show that they do most unequivocally acknowledge the same truths.

7. The Agency of the Holy Spirit in Conversion and Sanctification

The chief cause of misapprehension in regard to spiritual influence is, as it appears to me, to be found in the fact, that most persons confound the agency of the Spirit in the conversion of the sinner, with the influence he exerts as indwelling in the heart of the believer. Hence the vague and unscriptural notion, that the Spirit may be received before faith, and that faith itself is something wrought in the heart by a special and supernatural operation of the Spirit. This, indeed, seems to be, with many, the beginning and the end of all spiritual influence, and they depend, accordingly, upon certain mental or emotional impressions, of which they have once been the subjects, for their evidence of conversion, their assurance of pardon, their means of sanctification, and their hope of heaven.

We regard, however, the conversion of the sinner and sanctification of the believer, as distinct matters, accomplished, indeed, by the same Spirit, but in a different manner, and from a widely different position. We conceive the Holy Spirit to stand to the sinner in a relation very distinct from that in which he stands to him who is a member of the family of God. With the former, he is an outward witness for the truth; but the latter "has the witness in himself." To the first he is an unknown visitant or stranger; to the last, he is an indwelling and cherished guest. To the sinner, he is as the rain that falls upon the surface of the earth to soften and subdue. To the believer, he is as a fountain from within, springing up unto everlasting life.

In short, to bring the matter at once to issue, we deny that there is any scriptural authority for the notion that the unbeliever, or man of the world, can receive the Spirit of God. We hold this dogma to be in direct opposition to the Divine testimony, since Christ himself declares to his disciples that he would pray the Father, and He would give to them another Comforter, "even the Spirit of Truth," continues he, "WHOM THE WORLD CANNOT RECEIVE" (John 14.17).

That which is pure, must be received into a pure vessel. It is not until the heart is "purified by faith" that the Holy Spirit may enter to dwell therein. This is the view everywhere given in the Scriptures. Peter said to the believing penitents on the day of Pentecost, "Reform and be baptized for the remission of sins, and you shall [then] receive the gift of the Holy Spirit." Paul wrote to the Ephesians, "In Christ you also trusted, after that you heard the word of truth, the gospel of your salvation, in whom, also, after you believed, you were sealed with that Holy Spirit of promise, which is the earnest of our inheritance." And also to the Galatians: "Because you are sons, God has sent forth the Spirit of his Son into your hearts, crying Abba, Father." It is, on the other hand, nowhere stated that the Holy Spirit was given to any one to make him a believer, or a child of God.

But you may ask, is not every convert born of the Spirit? Must not every one be regenerated before entering the kingdom of heaven? True, but being "born of the Spirit," or regenerated, and receiving the Spirit, are matters quite different. No one can be born by receiving the Spirit. No one can be born of any thing that he receives; for the simple reason that he must be first born before he can receive any thing.

Hence the Scriptures say that the Spirit is given to those who "are sons." How, then, you will inquire, is an individual "born of the Spirit?" In order to comprehend this, we must be careful to maintain consistency in our interpretation of the figure, and must remember that, in the Scriptures, comparisons are employed with the utmost suitableness and accuracy, in illustration of the particular points to which they are applied.

The figure of a spiritual birth is drawn from a natural or literal birth—a re-generation from a generation. Hence, in all leading points, a just resemblance must be preserved between the fact and the figure. This we find, accordingly, in the language that the Scripture uses wherever this figure is introduced. James says, "God, according to his own will has begotten us by the word of truth." Peter says, we are "regenerated, not of corruptible seed, but incorruptible, even of the word of God, which lives and abides for ever." Paul says to the Corinthians: "Though you have ten thousand instructors in Christ, yet you do not have many fathers, for in Christ Jesus I have begotten you through the gospel." And John says: "Whosoever believeth that Jesus is the Christ, is begotten [born] of God."

It is the gospel, then, which constitutes the incorruptible seed of which the children of God are born. As in the parallel figure of the sower (Matt. 13), it is the gospel of the kingdom which is sown by the Son of man, and which, falling into good and honest hearts, brings forth abundant fruit to God. To believe that great proposition, that Jesus is the Christ, is, in John's expressive language, to be "begotten of God." It is thus with this sublime proposition and its proofs, as we formerly stated, that God first meets the sinner. In a word, it is the gospel that is received by the sinner, and not the Holy Spirit. Yet if he receive that gospel, spoken by the apostles in words inspired by the Holy Spirit, preached by them "with the Holy Spirit sent down from heaven," and "confirmed by demonstrations of the Spirit and of power," he is justly said to be "begotten of God," or of the Spirit, "through the word of truth."

When, at his baptism, he comes forth from the water as from the womb, the figure of regeneration is complete. He is born of water and Spirit.[1] He is born again "from above." Being thus born from above, he is prepared to receive that Spirit of adoption, that Holy Spirit or Comforter, which God bestows upon all his children, and which becomes to them an internal indwelling witness, and an earnest of their eternal inheritance, and produces in them, through its sanctifying influences and those of the truth it has revealed, the precious fruits of love, joy, peace, and righteousness.

The communication of the Holy Spirit may, then, be justly regarded as the great end of the ministration of the gospel. Unless the Holy Spirit be received and enjoyed, all faith, all forms, all professions are alike nugatory and vain. "If any man have not the Spirit of Christ, he is none of his," and consequently can have no heirship with him; no sonship to God; no earnest of a future inheritance. The possession of the Spirit is indeed the very evidence of sonship, and the proof that the gospel has been truly believed.

Nor is this enjoyment of the Holy Spirit momentary or transient in its nature, as many seem to think who mistake for it those evanescent excitements of feeling which may attend conversion. The Comforter is to abide with the Christian forever, and the latter is hence taught to seek "the supply of the Spirit of Christ." To ask, that he may receive. To seek, that he may find. To knock, that it may be opened to him. "For if you, being evil," said Christ to the disciples, "know how to give good gifts to your children, how much more shall hour heavenly Father give the Holy Spirit to them that ask him."

The graces and the blessedness of the Christian are alike "fruits of the Spirit." The peace of God which passes all understanding, and which keeps his heart and mind. The joy that animates, and the love which warms his soul, are inward feelings or emotions, which must be produced by the presence of the Divine Spirit, no less than those outward works of piety and humanity, which the gospel enjoins. The true kingdom of God, in short, is within the heart, and consists of "righteousness, peace, and joy in the Holy Spirit."

This, I presume, is a sufficient explanation of our views upon the subject legitimately before us. Obviously, there are various obstacles and hindrances that often prevent the gospel from reaching the heart of the sinner. There are, on the other hand, various agencies, ministerial and providential, human and Divine, general and special, which tend to remove these obstacles, and thus enable the gospel to exert its power, we freely admit. And hence it is necessary to seek these agencies, and proper to expect that God will, in answer to prayer, cause his word to be glorified in the conversion of those in whose behalf it is our duty and our privilege to ask his gracious interposition.

Nor do we deem it at all necessary that any controversy should exist with regard to the nature or mode of action of those influences that promote conversion. Certain it is that the same result will be effected, if these influences merely remove the impediments of ignorance, inattention, and love of the world, or any others which may obstruct the action of the gospel, as if they were to give such increased power and efficiency to the gospel itself, as to enable it to break through and overcome these obstacles.

If, as Paul intimates (2 Cor. 4.3,4), "the god of this world blinds by its perishing things the minds of those who believe not, lest the light of the glorious gospel of Christ should shine unto them," certainly those agencies which would simply remove the obstructions he interposes, would enable the light of the gospel to reach the heart of the sinner just as effectually as would an increase of light sufficient to penetrate these obstructions. It is not necessary that the light of the sun be increased a thousand fold in order that it may pierce the clouds that intercept it. All that is needed is for the clouds to be removed. Then the sun's beams will at once illuminate and warm whatever is thus exposed to them.

To say that the gospel requires a positive addition of power to enable it to reach the heart is to say that it is really deficient in power. But does not its power consist in the love of God that it reveals? How, then, could its power be augmented, unless by the addition of new facts, and nobler or more attractive views of God? But the gospel can receive no such addition, and consequently no increase of power. It is already "the power of God," and they who imagine it to have received additional power in their own experience, are unable to mention a single new fact or idea from which such additional power could be derived. But, as said before, it is quite unnecessary that any controversy should exist on the subject of converting influence. All should be content to preach the gospel and prayerfully commit the event to God, confident that though even a Paul may plant and an Apollos water, it is he alone that gives the increase.

As well might husbandmen neglect to sow their fields in order to debate with each other their respective theories in regard to the mode in which the seed is made to vegetate, as laborers of the Divine "husbandry," instead of preaching the gospel, occupy themselves with unprofitable discussions as to the mode in which God is pleased to render his word effective to salvation. We deprecate, therefore, the adoption of any theory upon this subject, and desire only to urge the claims of the gospel, as, at least, the only revealed instrumentality through which the Spirit of God accomplishes the conversion of the sinner. What influences he may exert in aid of the gospel, and in what particular manner the heart is "opened" for its reception, we regard as questions entirely subordinate, and as matters of opinion about which men may differ, without any just cause or occasion of disunion.

We deem it unfortunate, however, that any sentiments should gain currency in reference to this matter, which either, on the one hand, tend to depreciate and render ineffectual the word of God; or, on the other, represent God as a mere inactive spectator of the progress of the gospel. The Spirit of God is not to be separated from the word; neither is the word to be separated from the Spirit, in the great work of man's salvation. The former view opens the door to wild enthusiasm and every species of delusion. The latter view leads to a cold, abstract, undevotional philosophy, under whose influence true heartfelt religion declines and perishes.

That men are "regenerated by the incorruptible seed of the word," and sanctified 'through the truth," the Scripture distinctly affirms. Scripture also affirms that it is "the Spirit that quickens," and that Christians are God's "workmanship created in Christ Jesus unto good works." It should be sufficient for all reverently to believe these revealed truths, without presuming to theorize and dogmatize in regard to the particular mode in which either the word or the Spirit accomplishes the Divine purpose.

Note

1. Persons sometimes wonder why these words should be placed in this order, and why the water should not be mentioned last, since immersion follows, in order of time, the spiritual influence of the gospel. A moment's reflection, however, will show that this is the proper order, and the one actually most appropriate from the nature of the figure. A child, literally, must be born of its mother, before it can be said to be born of its father, and such is precisely the order of enunciation observed in the figure.

8. Weekly Communion

As we read in the Scriptures, that "on the first-day of the week the disciples came together to break bread;" and as the records show that it was the invariable custom of the early Christians to commemorate the death of Christ on every first-day of the week, we conceive that this order should be carefully maintained and attended to by all the churches now. We regard it as the great and special object of the Lord's Day meeting thus to commemorate the love of Christ, but it is usual to add prayer, exhortation, teaching, and so forth for mutual edification. Since pious and learned men of various parties have often deplored the departure of the modern churches from this ancient order of things, and have labored to restore the weekly observance of the Lord's Supper, we may justly regard the practice as sanctioned by the best authority, and its propriety placed beyond the reach of controversy.

From among those who have borne testimony upon this subject, I would adduce John Brown, of Haddington, who wrote a treatise upon it, in which he strongly advocated weekly communion. William King, also, Archbishop of Dublin, speaks as follows: "It is manifest that if it be not our own faults, we may have opportunity every Lord's day when we meet together, and, therefore, that church is guilty of laying aside the command, whose order and worship does not require and provide for this practice." Dr. Scott, in his commentary on Acts 20.7, says: "Breaking of bread, or commemorating the death of Christ in the Eucharist, was one chief end of their assembling; this ordinance seems to have been constantly administered every Lord's day."

Dr. Mason, of New York, asserts that, "Communion every Lord's day was universal, and was preserved in the Greek church till the seventh century."[1] Calvin complains of the neglect of this practice; "It ought to have been," says he, "far-otherwise. Every week, at least, the table of the Lord should have been spread for Christian assemblies, and the promises declared, by which, partaking of it, we might be spiritually fed."[2] John Wesley urged the same practice. In his letter to America, he says: "I also advise the elders to administer the supper of the Lord on every Lord's day."

Such, then, is the universal usage with us. We recognize, also, the importance of Sunday-schools and Bible classes for the instruction of the young. We also recognize the importance of wholly consecrating the Lord's day to the above purposes, as well as to private reading of the Scriptures and religious devotion.

Notes

1. Dr. John Mason's *Letter on Frequent Communion.*
2. *Inst.* Lib. 4. chap. 18, sect. 56.

9. Church Government

The Lord Jesus Christ, the great Shepherd of the flock, has committed the care of his church to pastors, or under-shepherds, who are commanded to "feed the flock of God," taking the oversight thereof, not be constraint, but willingly; not for filthy lucre, but of a ready mind. In the Scriptures, pastors are sometimes called bishops, or overseers, from the fact that they are usually possessed of age and experience. Their qualifications and duties are clearly stated in a number of places, including the letters to Timothy and Titus as well as in Paul's address to the elders of the church at Ephesus.

There should be a plurality of them in every church, as was evidently the case in primitive times. Paul addresses the church at Philippi, "with the bishops and deacons." Paul sent for the elders of the church at Ephesus, who seem, from his address to them, to have been a numerous body. Paul left Titus in Crete, to ordain elders in every city. There is no such thing recognized in Scripture as a bishop over a diocese, containing a plurality of churches. As to the arrogant pretensions of popes and prelates, who claim to come in place of the apostles, and to sit in the temple of God as representatives of Divinity, we find them only in the prophetic account that the apostles have given of the rise and development of the Man of Sin.

In the very nature of things, the apostles could have no successors. They were appointed by Christ in person, as his witnesses, and it was absolutely essential to their office, that they should have seen the Lord, and have had a personal knowledge of his resurrection from the dead. It was requisite, also, that they should have the power of working miracles, and other supernatural gifts, as proofs of their mission as Christ's ambassadors to the world. The gospel being fully delivered, and the testimony completed, this office could no longer continue. We recognize, accordingly, as rulers in the church, only the elders or overseers of each congregation, whose authority is restricted to the particular church by which they are chosen.

We have another class of officers, called deacons, whose duty it is to take charge of the temporal affairs of the church and minister to the sick, the poor, and the destitute. Evangelists or missionaries are also sustained by the churches, in the work of preaching the gospel to the world.

In Conclusion

I present to you, then, my dear friend, the preceding brief account of the chief matters urged upon the religious community in the present reformation movement. That Christian union can be affected by a return to the original principles of the gospel, and in no other way, is, I hope, by this time sufficiently evident. Simple principles, and not elaborate systems and doubtful opinions, must form the rallying point.

The fundamental principles of Protestantism, and the common Christianity of the religious world furnish, indeed, a present basis for the cooperation of all. Nothing is needed, with the Divine blessing, but the proper application of these principles, and the disentanglement of this common Christianity from the perplexed maze in which it is involved.

And oh! How desirable is a real Christian union in view of the present circumstances and future prospects of the church and the world. In the present rapid movements of society; in the spread of civilization; the increasing intercourse and fraternization of mankind; the opening of every region of the earth to missionary enterprise, and the manifest approach of the great day in which the Lord shall come to be "glorified in his saints," and to take vengeance on those "who know not God and obey not the gospel," how important that believers should present an unbroken front, and maintain that unity, without which, the conversion of the world and the perfection of the church, would seem to be alike impossible!

For Further Reading

Selected Writings by Robert Richardson

Communings in the Sanctuary. 1872. New edition. Orange, CA: New Leaf Books, 2000.

'Christian Unity—No. I." *Millennial Harbinger*, Fifth Series, 2 (February 1859), 64-69.

Memoirs of Alexander Campbell. 2 volumes. 1868.

"Nature of the Christian Doctrine—No. I." *Millennial Harbinger* 4th series, 6 (April 1856), 198-204.

"Our Creed—Is It Evangelical?" *Christian Standard* (2 January 1869), 1.

"Reformation—No. I." *Millennial Harbinger*, Third Series, 4 (May 1847), 275-279.

"Reformation—No. II." *Millennial Harbinger*, Third Series, 4 (June 1847), 313-316.

"Reformation—No. IV." *Millennial Harbinger*, Third Series, 4 (September 1847), 503-509.

A Scriptural View of the Office of the Holy Spirit. 1872.

"Spirituality of the Gospel." *Millennial Harbinger*, Third Series, 7 (June 1850), 314-320.

"Union of Christians." *Millennial Harbinger* 37 (March 1866), 97-101.

Selected Writings about Robert Richardson

Allen, C. Leonard, and Danny Swick. *Participating in God's Life: Two Theological Crossroads for Churches of Christ*. Orange, CA: New Leaf Books, 2000.

Allen, C. Leonard. *Distant Voices: Discovering a Forgotten Past for a Changing Church*. Abilene: TX: ACU Press, 1993. Pages 70-76.

Berry, Stephen P. "Room for the Spirit: The Contribution of Robert Richardson." *Lexington Theological Quarterly* 21 (July 1986), 81-90.

Brooks, Pat. "Robert Richardson: Nineteenth Century Advocate of Spirituality." *Restoration Quarterly* 21 (1978), 135-49.

Goodnight, Cloyd and Dwight E. Stevenson. *Home to Bethphage: A Biography of Robert Richardson*. St. Louis: Christian Board of Publication, 1949.

Also Available

The first and greatest work of devotion in the Stone-Campbell movement

COMMUNINGS IN THE SANCTUARY

ROBERT RICHARDSON

Introduced and Edited by C. Leonard Allen

NEW LEAF BOOKS

"To open *Communings in the Sanctuary* is to enter a vast, largely unexplored, field of 19th century piety. It comes as something of a shock to those who thought they knew their spiritual roots to find a book so completely animated by the love of God and the mystery of God... Taken slowly and meditatively, these masterpieces are sure to awaken the soul tot he joys of devotion."
Darryl Tippens, Provost, Pepperdine University

148 pages, $11.95 paper
To order call toll free 1-877-634-6004

New Leaf Books